DEMOCRATISATION PROCESS IN NORTH-EAST INDIA

DEMOCRATISATION PROCESS IN NORTH-EAST INDIA

Some Issues and Challenges

Edited by
S. Thianlalmuan Ngaihte,
L.T. Sasang Guite

GYAN

ISBN: 978-81-212-1236-6

Price: ₹ 850

First Published, 2015

Published by

Gyan Publishing House
23, Main Ansari Road
Daryaganj, New Delhi-110002
Phones: 23282060, 23261060
Fax: 91-11-23285914
E-mail: books@gyanbooks.com

Laser Typesetting: Gyan Print (AB-I), Delhi
Printed at: Chawla Offset Printers, Delhi

Cataloging in Publication Data—DK
Courtesy: D.K. Agencies (P) Ltd. <docinfo@dkagencies.com>

"Democratisation Process and the Zomis" (Seminar) (2013 : Shillong, India)

Democratisation process in North-East India : some issues and challenges/ editors, S. Thianlalmuan Ngaihte, L.T. Sasang Guite.

p. cm.

Includes bibliographical references and index.

ISBN 9788121212366

1. Democratization—India, Northeastern—Congresses. 2. India, Northeastern—Scheduled tribes—Politics and government—Congresses. 3. India, Northeastern—Politics and government—Congresses. 4. Gender mainstreaming—India, Northeastern—Congresses. 5. Identity politics—India, Northeastern—Congresses. I. Ngaihte, S. Thianlalmuan, 1979- II. Guite, L. T. Sasang. III. Title.

DDC 320.9541 23

Contents

Foreword

This edited book is a culmination of the two-day national seminar, organised by Siamsinpawlpi (SSPP) (*Reg. No. 1107 of 1972 of the Society Acts XXI of 1860*), Joint Headquarters, Shillong during 19-20 March 2013. It was organised as a part of its golden jubilee celebration (GJC), where I was the Chairman of the GJC Committee, and the theme of the seminar was "Democratisation Process and the Zomis". The seminar was held at the Conference Hall of Indian Council of Social Science Research-North Eastern Regional Centre (ICSSR-NERC), NEHU campus, Shillong and was sponsored by the ICSSR, New Delhi and ICSSR-NERC, Shillong. S. Thianlalmuan Ngaihte and L.T. Sasang Guite, editors of the book, were Coordinators of the seminar.

The seminar had participants from different disciplines and diverse backgrounds, which is evident from the names of the contributors to this volume. The papers presented at the seminar delved into many aspects of democratisation process and various emerging issues concerning the Zomis, in particular, and the tribals of North-East, in general. I am pleased to all the contributors for their insightful papers, and to the President, SSPP for giving freedom to the organisers of the seminar for publication of this edited book.

We could not have undertaken the publication of the papers without support of Gyan Publishing House, New Delhi.

There are hundreds of books on the French and American Revolutions, or Indian freedom struggle: biographies of their leaders, studies of the social background of the protagonists and fall out. In contrast, the works by scholars on political movements in NE India can be counted on the fingers. As such, compiling of this kind of book on democratic issues among the tribes of the region would go a long way in not only opening up the minds of policy makers but also in helping the administrators in taking appropriate political decisions.

I am extremely happy to the editors for their careful editing of the book. I hope the book will find its rightful place in the academic circles and capture attention among scholars and academicians.

Shillong
January 2014

T.K. Hangzo, IDAS
Integrated Financial Adviser
Eastern Air Command
Shillong

Preface

This book contained a thoroughly revised version of papers presented during the two-day national seminar that was held on 19-20 March 2013 at the Conference Hall of ICSSR-NERC, NEHU campus, Shillong. We also requested select scholars to write on issues related to the theme of the book.

The objectives of this edited book is :

- To highlight the importance for democratising gender equality.
- To understand democratisation vis-à-vis identity politics/civil society/state.
- To see if the age-old traditions and practices of communities hinder operation of democratic principles and system. That is, whether customary laws and practices, and traditional institutions are democratic enough in their structures and functions.
- To highlight some challenges to process of democratisation in the North-East (NE).

All works, views and findings of the authors are their own. The editors do not take any responsibility for the views expressed by the authors and/or the findings made by them.

We thank Dr. C.J. Thomas, Deputy Director, ICSSR-NERC, Shillong for his constant support. We are grateful to ICSSR, New Delhi and ICSSR-NERC for sponsoring the seminar. We also express our gratitude to all the contributors for responding positively to the editorial suggestions.

The paper by S. Thianlalmuan Ngaihte gives a preliminary reading on democratisation and briefly presents some challenges to the process of democratisation. Toki Blah highlights some pertinent issues/challenges faced by contemporary NE tribal communities.

The second section of the book is on "gender issues". There

are four papers where each contributor highlights the need for democratising gender equality. As an anthropologist, Lucy T.V. Zehol presents an anthropological perspective on gender. She pointed out that anthropological studies have highlighted cross-cultural variations in human behaviour, social structure and beliefs/meaning of systems, which helped attract attention to the social and historical specificity of the notion of gender and denied their having an ontological or biological basis. Zehol takes the Zomi of NE as a case study to support her arguments.

Tara Manchin Hangzo sees gender as a concept that has to do with the perception and mindset and the significant changes in attitudes and impact on traditional roles for both genders. She identifies some contentious or critical indicators relating to gender equality and explores if gender equality is realised and achieved in her community.

As a woman and someone who writes on and about women of in NE India, Ninglun Hanghal sees indigenous communities' "way of life" — culture, customs, traditions, practices and socio-political systems as highly patriarchal in nature. Though formal education, democratic constitutions and legal provisions paved the way for women to come out in demand for a rightful space, the gender divide and perception of gender roles continues to play out in various forms.

Lalgin Chongloi presents the patriarchal nature of Kuki society where women were subjugated and alienated. His paper shows that gender inequality is played out in property and law of inheritance where customary law always favours the male.

The third section is on "democratisation *vis-a-vis* identity politics/civil society/state". Contemporary NE India has witnessed critical role played by ethnic issues in shaping the politics of the region. Ethnic politics has a direct bearing on issues of democratisation in the region. Akhil Ranjan Dutta argues that assertion of identity around ethnicity and culture was perceived as a potential force towards democratisation of the regimented perception of nation and the nation-state. On the basis of the UNDP's Annual Human Development

Report, 2004 and others, Dutta pointed out the critical role played by cultural identity in building both democracy and human development. However, as culture operates in given social-political frameworks, it has its own contradictions. Identities around culture and ethnicity are attempted to be used for political mileage both by the state and by the emerging elites from within (those) ethno-cultural communities. To support his arguments, Dutta critically analyses inter-linkages between identity politics and democratisation as manifested in Bodoland in Assam.

In a similar, yet different vein, Gorky Chakraborty talks about the emerging reality of identity issues in the NE, wherein he pointed out the unique experience of NE's transformation from politicisation of ethnicity to ethnicisation of politics. He wonders if this transformation is a pattern of changing of the pre-modern to the modern. Are ethnic movements in NE India, a manifestation of the effort of the neglected population groups towards a fair accommodation in the nation-state framework? Has democratisation released the latent potential among these population groups towards their aspiration for a space within the nation-state? Gorky analyses these issues within the broader framework of nation-tribe dichotomisation in the NE.

We often think that civil society is inclusive in their operations, not just limited to one tribal/community issues. This point of view is refuted by Roluahpuia, wherein he sees civil society in NE India as the "vanguard" of ethno-political aspiration and articulation. When civil society in the NE are found to be extremely ethnically exclusivist in their perception and operations, the challenges before them is upholding the democratic spirit and democratisation process.

H. Kamkhenthang and Asok Kumar Ray highlight the nature of democracy in the Zomi political system and the various agents/forces that have influenced and shaped their democratic discourse, and their social and political aspirations. They argued that the Zomis keep on democratic norms by adopting rules, regulations and byelaws which are democratic in nature.

Next, we have "peace education", where Leban Serto talks about the need to promote democracy and peace education in the NE. In order to overcome ethnic problems/conflicts, it becomes necessary to have a concrete strategy, and one such step is the need to invest for peace building which is so much required for the region. Democratic process and peace education are interlinked and need to go side by side in building of democratic atmosphere.

The last section of the book is "beyond the horizon", where each contributor focusses on issues that are directly or indirectly related to democratisation, or the need for a paradigm shift for progress and development. Pum Khan Pau's paper provides insight into the making of colonial "agent" in Chin Hills. Being a leader in the socio-economic, political and religious life of the people, the chief in Zo society became the focus of the British when they colonised Chin Hills. By redefining the traditional authority and functions of the chief, the colonial administration succeeded in making the chief(s) as an "agent" of "indirect rule".

Valte Vungzamuan looks ethnic aspirations from a development perspective and unveils the implication of ethnic aspirations/politics on the socio-economic development of the tribes of Manipur.

Ginlianlal Buhril highlights challenges of democratisation process in India's NE through a case study of the Zomi community. He calls for a shift in perspective. That is, focus must be on the self, others, society and business and that better leadership and governance can be learned. The last article by R. Sanga talks about tribal land issues of Manipur.

We shall feel honoured if this book is of any help to students, scholars and academicians, and public and community leaders who are one of the main actors of the democracy.

Shillong, 2014

S. Thianlalmuan Ngaihte,
L.T. Sasang Guite

List of Contributors

Toki Blah (toki@neline.com) is a social activist, columnist and President of Informed Conscious and Responsible Existence (ICARE), an NGO based in Shillong.

Lucy T.V. Zehol (lzehol@yahoo.com) is a Professor in the Department of Anthropology, North-Eastern Hill University, Shillong.

Tara Manchin Hangzo (taramanchin@gmail.com), an Independent Health Consultant, has worked for 16 years in the social development sector, mainly in the HIV IDU TI sector. She worked basically with international funding organisations such as Action Aid India, HIV/AIDS Alliance, Project Concern International, AIF (American India Foundation) DEVPRO and WHO and Emmanuel Hospital Association and the UN agencies.

Ninglun Hanghal (hanghal.ninglun@gmail.com) is a New Delhi based freelance journalist. She contributes to *The Sangai Express,* Manipur daily newspaper as its Delhi correspondent.

Lalgin Chongloi (lalgin@yahoo.com) teaches Sociology at Raid Laban College, Shillong.

Akhil Ranjan Dutta (akhilranjangu@gmail.com) is an Associate Professor in the Department of Political Science, Gauhati University, Guwahati.

Gorky Chakraborty (gorky8bob@gmail.com) primarily works on development issues related to North-East India. He divides his career between teaching and research. He has worked on the chars (river islands) of Brahmaputra for his doctoral thesis and dealt with the Look East Policy as a post-doctoral fellow. Presently, he is with the Institute of Development Studies Kolkata (IDSK).

Roluahpuia (puite.tiss@gmail.com) is presently pursuing integrated MPhil and PhD work at Tata Institute of Social Sciences (TISS), Guwahati.

Leban Serto (leban.serto@gmail.com) is presently the Coordinator, Peace Studies Department at Martin Luther Christian University, Shillong, India.

Pum Khan Pau (puapau@gmail.com) is an Assistant Professor in the Department of History, Visva Bharati University, Santiniketan, West Bengal.

Valte Vungzamuan, IRS (v_valte@rediffmail.com) is presently working in the Government of India, Ministry of Finance, Department of Revenue.

H. Kamkhenthang (drkamkhenthang@yahoo.com) is a retired Director of Tribal Research Institute, Manipur.

Asok Kumar Ray (ashokray.ray280@ gmail.com) is a scholar on North-East India. Presently, he is a Visiting Fellow at OKD Institute of Social Change and Development, Guwahati.

Ginlianlal Buhril (gbuhril12@rediffmail.com) is a Professor of Management (Human Resources Management and Organisational Behaviour) at the Universal Business School, Karjat, Mumbai. He is also the Director Corporate Governance and Head of the MBA Programme with the Cardiff Metropolitan University, UK.

R. Sanga (rsanga_05@yahoo.co.in) was a student leader earlier, and now a social activist and writer.

SECTION–I: PRELUDE

1

Democratisation: Preliminary Reading

S. Thianlalmuan Ngaihte

Scholars talk about the wave of democratisation. For instance, the "third wave" (Huntington 1991) of democratisation began in the seventies and swept across the developing countries in the eighties and nineties. Originated in southern Europe, the third democratisation wave moved to Latin America, Asia and Africa in due course. During the third wave period, the nature of regimes' transformation from undemocratic to democratic system was remarkable. In 1974, there were 41 democracies among the existing 150 states in the world. By 2003, about three-fifth states were considered formal democracies (Rakner et. al. 2007: 7). According to Boutros-Ghali, "Democratisation is a process which leads to a more open, more participatory, less authoritarian society. Democracy is a system of government, which embodies, in a variety of institutions and mechanisms, the ideal of political power based on the will of the people" (1996: 1).

Democratisation as a process is said to have gone through three phases, *viz.*, the liberalisation phase, a transition phase and the consolidation phase. In the first phase, authoritarian regime opens up or crumbles. The second phase often begins when the first competitive elections are held. Finally, in the last phase, democratic practices are firmly established and accepted by most relevant actors (O'Donnell and Schmitter 1986; Linz and Stepan 1996).

According to Schumpeter (1942), a democratic method is "that institutional arrangement for arriving at political decisions in which individuals acquire the power to decide by means of a competitive struggle for the people's vote". Elaborating Schumpeter's definition, Dahl (1971) points out the following essentials for democracy: "(i) Control over governmental decisions about policy constitutionally vested in elected officials; (ii) Relatively frequent, fair and free elections, (iii) Universal adult suffrage; (iv) The right to run for public office; (v) Freedom of expression; (vi) Access to alternative sources of information that are not monopolised by either the government or any other single group; and (vii) Freedom of association" (cited in Rakner et. al. 2007: 6).

A number of democratisation scholars came out with more substantive definition of democracy where accountability matters the most. They strongly argued that the process of democratisation is not just a transition to formal democracy but also consolidation of democratic system. The accountabilities, they considered important, are vertical accountability, horizontal accountability and societal accountability. The first one enables citizens to hold their political leaders to account through the electoral channel. The second one is the presence of accountability mechanisms within the distinct bodies of government itself, whereby state institutions are authorised and willing to oversee, control, redress and, if need be, sanction unlawful actions by other state institutions (O'Donnell 1996). The last accountability refers to the (ongoing) watchdog functions of civic associations and an independent mass media over the actions of the state (Schedler et. al. 1999).

What can be inferred from the above is that the democratisation process is about transformation of non-democratic political regime(s)/structure(s) into a more inclusive democratic system and further consolidation of the same. Democracy as "government by the people" is all about the institutionalisation of people power. Interpretation of democracy as related to elections is a global trend which the evangelists of democracy have tirelessly tried to spread (democracy) across the world (Rakner et. al. 2007: 6).

The opening up of an autocratic or authoritarian political regime or feudal state to a democratic system, no doubt, provides political space to people, which enables the masses preferences to shape public policy. As democracy is about empowering citizens of all backgrounds, the right to vote alone is not sufficient to accomplish this. True democracy goes beyond suffrage (Welzel and Inglehart 2008: 127). Even though Dahl's definition of formal democracy includes the basic civil liberties that guarantee inclusive democratic process, it is still criticised on electoral grounds. For a long time, it was assumed that "elections will be not just a foundation-stone but a key generator over time of further democratic reforms" (Carothers 2002).

Democratic discourse should not take into account only the political aspects but also those social/cultural institutions and practices of societies/communities, which do not conform to the contemporary democratic principles. The socio-cultural issues cannot be separated from the political aspects. All of them, directly or indirectly, affect the private and public space of the members of the society.

We all know that "democratisation" is a very broad concept, which goes beyond periodic elections and representative government. It covers social, economic and cultural issues of our daily life and activities. For the disadvantaged or neglected section of societies/communities, it may even mean the ways one think, feel and speak in relation to others. That is, interpersonal relationship that one always performs in their daily lives.

If democracy is an encompassing concept, the pillars of democracy—right, liberty and equality—should also be an encompassing one, not only in theory, but in application as well. They are prerequisites for establishing a democratic space/atmosphere. It allows people to participate in the activities of society and politics without any discrimination based on gender, class, ethnic backgrounds, colour, etc. A democratic culture allows people the freedom to express themselves, to choose their ways of life and personal preferences in governing their private lives and to make their political preferences count in governing public life. This, no doubt, is what democracy implies and what democratisation process should try to achieve.

Can There ever be Absolute Democratisation

When can we say that democratisation process has succeeded or failed? This is a very difficult question to answer, where, I suppose, there can be contradictory answers to it. Democratisation process will have no ending. Human beings' desire for democratising everything that affects their life and preferences will continue to grow. As people become more conscious of their self-identity and their place in the social, cultural and political set-up, they also become more vocal in asserting and articulating their democratic right and freedom. So long as human beings exist in this world, the democratisation process will continue.

We all know that rights, liberty and equality are not absolute. They are conditioned by social good. Individual rights need to be protected against arbitrary state/society actions. The state/society also needs safeguards from violent/ undemocratic actions of individual(s). How can individual rights, group rights and state/society's interests be reconciled? Though a democratic state and society is bound by democratic norms and principles, the stark question that will continue to stare at us is, can there ever be absolute democratisation?

To answer this question, let me take up the strong belief that I used to subscribed to. I used to believe that the solution to India's diverse problems, especially political one, could be found in her Constitution. And I used to argue that India's democratic ideals, philosophy, its institutions and form of government, and her legal system are sufficient enough to deal with the diverse voices of dissent and protest in a democratic manner. However, I was wrong. The big challenge that is unlikely to materialise is - can the democratic ideals and philosophy enshrined in the Preamble and the Indian Constitution be ever carried out in letter and spirit?

While this is not beyond human's imagination, it is outside man's power to fulfill. Men are rational beings, yet the means they employ to fulfill their interests may not always justify the end. In other words, the decisions and actions of all rational beings may not always be rational. With so many actors of diverse backgrounds and interests playing their role within the social, economic and political set up, it may not be (always) possible on the part of the state/society to deliver justice to each player. Moreover, the state also has its own interest to protect and safeguard – sometimes it may be driven by her security interests, at another time may be by communal forces, vote bank politics, market forces and the forces of globalisation, etc.

Related to all these challenges are the unlimited wants of human beings and the limited resources of the state/society at their disposal. Human/ethnic aspirations will never cease to exist. Today, we may be able to provide the wants of a person/ ethnic group, or we may be able to solve problems of one person/ethnic group. Even then, there is no guarantee that problem of the same nature will not erupt again in the future. Instead, sooner or later, problem of the same kind is likely to crop up from/in the social and political milieu because the desires of one human being are no different from that of others.

"The essential value of democracy is presumed to lie in its moral superiority over any other way of arriving at decisions which take everybody's interest into account, and are equally binding on everyone" (Jayal 2009: 2). Democracy makes possible a just and free society, through the apparatus of rights and freedoms. Nevertheless, the enabling conditions for such public action may not be there in all societies/ communities. Also, human beings may agree on the purpose of their collective endeavour, yet they will surely disagree about the methods of achieving it (*Ibid*: xxiv). Ultimately, it is one's conscience, understanding and action commensurate to collective good that matters the most.

Scholars, community leaders/elites, institutions and organisations often claimed to be the champion of rights and freedoms that India's democracy entails. The fact is that, even those claiming to represent the masses, poor, etc., often ignored the lack of internal democracy in the social and political organisations/institutions, etc., they (claim to) represent.

Some Select Challenges to Democratisation Process

Challenges to the process of democratisation can come from gender issues, customary norms and practices, ethno-political aspirations, civil society, etc.

Democratising Gender Equality

The family and gender relations constitute an important field of democratisation. In a society where gender roles are determined by customary norms and practices, men become the centre of everything. Elsewhere in other parts of the world, societies in North-East are patriarchal in nature. Representation and decision-making, be it in the family, ethnic organisations, social and political institutions, etc., are dominated by males, and are almost the prerogative of men. In such a social and political set-up, what does democratisation have to do with gender equality?

In spite of women's remarkable contributions in all spheres of life in the society, they continue to be subjugated. One of the greatest barriers for achieving a democratised gender atmosphere is our attitude and perception coloured by the social and cultural baggage that we inherited from our past.

How democratic an institution/organisation is, can be known by the extent of representation, status and power enjoyed by both the genders. A democratic society/system devoid of gender equality is an imperfect democracy. It is important to democratise gender equality.

Tradition Versus Democratic Principles

This issue deserves close examination. In a democratic political and legal set-up, such as India, modern democratic institutions and system exist side by side with traditional institutions and system where customary norms and practices hold sway. The operation of both systems of institutions and governance complements each other in many areas, while it can be a problem for the normal functioning of the two in certain cases.

In other words, sometimes it is the traditional norms and practices which prevail over liberal democratic principles and the vice-versa. While this is a positive thing that should be appreciated, the question that needs to be asked is, whether democratic system is a threat to age-old traditions and practices of the communities, or can we say that traditional values interfere with democratic governance that professes the rule of law.

What is modern and democratic for someone may be very much traditional for others. What is traditional for some people may still be democratic/modern for others. Can we call all contemporary remnants of tradition or customary practices undemocratic/un-modern? Ultimately, what is important is to have a balanced democratisation process which will bridge tradition and modernity, and where the rights and liberty of individuals are protected, but not at the expense of collective good.

Ethno-political Aspirations

Reorganisation of states (provinces) in India can be seen as one of the outcomes of democratisation process in the country. To accommodate political aspirations and movements by communities/nationalities in India, states were reorganised on linguistic and ethnic lines. In the context of North-East

India, the Indian state reorganised the region on ethnic lines and also introduced Sixth Schedule in the Indian Constitution to administer some of the tribal dominated areas of the region. Even then, ethnic movements and demands for autonomy/ homeland continue to survive. Competing ethnic political goals in the North-East directly or indirectly affect democratic discourses in the region. It affects peaceful co-existence of people, economic progress and development.

Should the Indian state again re-organise the region in order to accommodate ethnic demands for autonomy/ homeland? If so, will another re-organisation of the region be the ultimate solution to ethnic aspirations/politics? My submission would be, if re-organising the NE on ethnic lines were the solution to her crisis, ethnic political aspirations would have been nipped in the bud long back.

Are there alternative policies or steps that the Indian state can resort to? This is a valid political question that deserves to be discussed and debated upon by all concerned persons and authorities. I personally believe that there are many policy alternatives available to the Indian state. One such step can be giving more power to the existing Autonomous District Councils in all the states of the region, or granting Sixth Schedule status to those areas where the people aspire for. Such a step, if followed, would be just an internal (re)adjustment of boundaries within the state(s), which will not disintegrate but safeguard the territorial integrity of the existing states (provinces) of the region. Another functional step is to strengthen the efficiency of governmental and administrative machinery at the state, local and grassroots levels. Moreover, it is also necessary to check corruption and see that development funds/packages reach the target people/ group. I will address this issue in details in other context.

It will be suffice for me to say that it is always good on the part of Indian State to be sensitive to the political aspirations of communities/nationalities. It is also important to know that promoting democratic culture, that seeks to protect diversity (of the North-East), rather than promote exclusive ethnic interests, would be always beneficial for the people and the region.

Democratisation Process and Civil Society

One of the prerequisites for building a democratic society is creating and safeguarding space for civil society. Civil society was treated as synonymous with or even a precondition for democratisation. While some argued that democracy and freedom are necessary for a vibrant civil society, others claimed that a vibrant civil society is itself an essential condition for consolidating democracy (Jayal 2009: 18).

Challenges to civil society can come from the state, the society and from within itself. As a bridge between the state and the society, civil society cannot be partial in their operation. They are expected to monitor, analyse and lobby for changes to government policies. Nevertheless, they are also expected to be critical to both—to the policies and action of the government and the society they represent.

Conclusion

Democratisation process goes far beyond suffrage and representation. It is also concerned with the social, economic and cultural issues and activities of human life. As a process, democratisation continues to face challenges in representing the conscious voices of all sections of the society/community, in bridging gender divide, in responding to diverse genuine voices of dissent in a democratic manner, and in upholding the very democratic values and ideals that democracy stands for.

The state has to safeguard its security and interest. The society too has to protect its interests from the arbitrary action of the state and individual. The individual too has the same interest in fulfilling his/her personal interest. Though absolute democratisation is impossible to achieve, it may be possible to have an ideal democratic atmosphere and culture. It is expected that a democratic state and society allows people the freedom to express themselves, to choose their way of life and personal preferences in governing their private life, to make their political preferences count in governing public life. Individual, people, societies and institutions/ organisations in a democratic state are expected to response to the issues and challenges in a democratic manner. It is desired that the rights of all citizens, for instance, enshrined in Part III of the Indian Constitution—right to equality, right to freedom, cultural rights, right to constitutional remedies, etc.—inspire all actors.

References

Boutros-Ghali, Boutros (1996): *An Agenda for Democratization* (New York: United Nations Department of Public Information).

Carothers, T. (2002): "The End of the Transition Paradigm", *Journal of Democracy,* 13(1): 1-21.

Dahl, R.A. (1971): *Polyarchy: Participation and Opposition* (New Haven, CT: Yale University Press).

Jayal, Niraja Gopal ed. (2009): *Democracy in India* (Oxford: Oxford University Press).

Linz, J. and A. Stepan (1996): *Problems of Democratic Transition and Consolidation: Southern Europe, South America and Post-Communist Europe* (Baltimore, MD: Johns Hopkins University Press).

O'Donnell, G. and P. Schmitter (1986): *Transitions from Authoritarian Rule: Tentative Conclusions about Uncertain Democracies* (Baltimore, MD: Johns Hopkins University Press).

O'Donnell, G. (1996): "Illusions about Consolidation", *Journal of Democracy,* 7(2): 34-51.

Rakner, Lise, Alina Rocha Menocal and Verena Fritz (2007): *"Democratisation's Third Wave and the Challenges of Democratic Deepening: Assessing International Democracy Assistance and Lessons Learned",* Working Paper 1, Research project (RP-05-GG) of the Advisory Board for Irish Aid, August.

Schedler, A., L. Diamond and M.F. Plattner (1999): *The Self-restraining State: Power and Accountability in New Democracies* (Boulder, CO: Lynne Rienner).

Schumpeter, J. (1942): *Capitalism, Socialism and Democracy* (London: Harper Perennial).

Welzel, Christian and Ronald Inglehart (2008): "The Role of Ordinary People in Democratisation", *Journal of Democracy,* January, 19(1): 126-140.

2

Thought on Challenges of Democratisation among Tribals of North-East India

Toki Blah

There is a common feature that runs across the indigenous upland people of North-East (NE) India. The rest of India prefers to call them the tribals of the NE. No matter what, the fact remains that most of the tribes in NE are Tibeto-Burman in lineage, except for the Khasis and Jaintias of Meghalaya state who are of Austro-Asian descent. The tribals of NE are people, diverse in their ethnic minority existence. Diverse as individual tribes or communities, yet similar to each other in their socio-cultural make-up, and aspirations as far as their world views are concerned. What we, therefore, speak about the larger entity will apply too to the smaller entity that belongs to NE.

Another common feature of the indigenous people of NE is that all of them have been caught up in the turmoil of development. All of them speak of the need for development, or of the lack of it, or of its total absence. Development is a common issue for all the people of the region. Yet, development is one of the least understood words that have ever been uttered in the region.

We continue to measure development by the Western standards. We define its existence or absence by infrastructure of roads, houses, bridges, schools, etc., or in the rise or absence in Gross Domestic Product. Is this really the meaning of development or are these simply aspects that contribute to development?

Development for the North-East should be defined within the context of the NE tribal. Development should be seen as the process of transformation of tribal society from one level to another. For the people of the region, this transformation began more than 150 years ago. It started when the traditional form of oral communication gave way to the written word. It totally transformed and changed their way of life. This process of change is still continuing when recently the written form mutated into the digital form of communication. It completely changed their concept of wisdom and knowledge.

Knowledge, wisdom and the ability to survive as a community is no longer linked to the experience of old age. Today, academic qualifications, technological skills and political endowments are the instruments of change that we associate with superior knowledge. It is this that will guide the tribals of NE into the future.

The indigenous communities of the NE have started to shift their socio-political goal posts. Pre-occupation with local and traditional issues has yielded way to an increasing interest on issues outside their immediate localities. Tribal NE communities can now safely claim to have a world-view of their own, a world-view that they are increasingly sharing with other indigenous communities the world wide. We can say that transformation is once again overtaking the tribal communities or that transformation is an ongoing process. It has not been easy for the communities because change or transformation can be traumatic, especially for isolated and remote minorities of the NE. Nevertheless, it is necessary for the communities of the region to come to terms with the challenge of change.

A closer look at the transformed tribal society, we speak of, shows that they have also begun the process of asking very uncomfortable questions about themselves, their correlation with others and the future of their identity, so much so that the politics of identity has become a permanent fixture in their socio-political make-up. The process of introspection within their respective communities is a purging and churning exercise. Of relevance, perhaps, are the questions we have started asking ourselves about:

- Relevance of tradition and traditional institutions *vis-á-vis* provisions of the Constitution such as the 73rd and 74th Amendments to the Constitution. These constitutional provisions provide the people of India with platforms to enact participatory forms of governance at the grassroots level. They include the concepts of transparency and accountability in public life. They advocate the inclusion of women in all community decision-making exercises. They mirror the modern trends towards efficacious democratic practices. Unfortunately, they also pose challenges to the traditional forms of governance. It is a process of change that the tribals in the North-East are often confronted with.
- Cultural identity is another challenge that most NE tribals face as they move towards better and modern practices of democratisation. They are often caught up between culture and identity. Often, aspects like the clothes they wear, the languages they speak, the festivals they celebrate are identified as the culture and identity of a community. They ignored/forgot that perhaps, the above, singly or collectively, are mere expressions of culture. They catch the eye because of their sentimental, emotional and easily quantifiable qualities, but they do not necessarily embody the culture or identity of any community. In the process, the NE tribals tend to forget the intrinsic value systems that determine the tribal way of life—value systems that really define their identities.
- Gender equality is another important issue that needs to be looked into. Most tribal societies revere their

women so far as their status as mothers and sisters is concerned. In the same breath, they are convulsed over the question of women empowerment. Paradoxically, they have no issues over constitutional empowerment of women but, at the same time, carry traditional reservations in giving women space in decision-making platforms. It is a paradox that the North-East tribals are still struggling with.

- The world is facing major challenges from climate change and globalisation. Humanity is apprehensive of the former while unsure of the latter. Indigenous people, the world over, hold potential and workable solutions as far as the climate change is concerned. The forte of tribals is their equation with nature and the answers they can provide against carbon invasion. At the same time, the challenges of globalisation appear threatening and invasive to the tribal way of life. They are torn apart between the two. Democratisation seems to provide a way out, but how, is yet to be determined.
- All tribals of the NE struggle with another enigma not unsimilar to that of "the egg and the chicken". It is the question of conflict or peace. The issue before them is which is the most relevant to their needs. It is a question that is still blowing in the wind for most of them.

This is the state of affairs that the tribals of the NE find themselves in. They have major questions and issues that are directly connected with their future. Problem is that answers to these questions can no longer be the prerogative of elders. Neither can they be the privilege of males only. Then there is the whole question of feudalism and customary patronage that have become outmoded and archaic. It becomes necessary to find answers to the above through participative and inclusive socio-political paradigms. The people are starting to probe, to question and to ask, if this is not the churning process of democratisation, then what it is?

In conclusion, I think, I have tried to answer, perhaps some of the issues relevant to NE tribal communities. The indigenous people of the NE, irrespective of their ethnic make-up, face a common challenge–the need to change and transform within a new world order. Over 150 years ago, they met the challenges of change and yet, they are still under the process of that transformation. Today, they are again faced with fresh instances for a need to undergo, yet, another process of change. The challenges of globalisation, of opening up, of climate change, of the need to look beyond the borders of their villages, towns and region are ready to face them.

Where will the answer lie? In democratisation of the Western concepts or in their traditional comfort zones? Or will it lie in their ability to amalgamate the two?

SECTION–II: GENDER ISSUES

3

An Anthropological Perspective on Gender

Lucy T.V. Zehol

Gender: A Conceptual Discussion

It is only within fairly recent history that the meaning and significance which cultures and societies assign to feninity and masculinity have been questioned. And gender has become a category of social analysis. While emphasising the possibility of multiple ways of conceptualising, experiencing, "performing" or "doing gender", R.W. Connell offers the working definition of "gender" in his book, *Gender* (2002: 10) as, "the structure of social relations that centres on the reproductive arena, and the set of practices (governed by this structure) that brings reproductive distinction between bodies into social processes". In this definition, "gender" is intimately linked with meanings and interpretations of reproductions and sexual bodies, but expands beyond that realm to structure other social processes as in Mauss' terminology, gender could be given the status of a "total social fact".

In everyday conversation, however, the term "gender" may more often be used interchangeably with "sex" as a categorical reference. That is, "male" and "female" which are two examples of "gender". The distinction between "sex" and "gender" as analytical categories can be traced back to developments in sociological, medical sciences and social/

cultural anthropology of the 20th century. Simone de Beauvoir's (1949), political criticism of the subordination of women, entitled *The Second Sex,* linked the cultural devaluation of women in Western society to biological differences between men and women. Gayle Rubin (1975: 157-210), explored the notion of a sex or gender system, whereby the "raw resources" of male and female bodies become "gendered" products through processes of socialisation, normative behaviours, hegemonic representation, etc.

The "raw resources" referred to by Rubin were defined by a conception of bio-medical differences between "male" and "female", research on chromosomes, gonads, differences between the genitals, hormones, brain size and psychology (men have more grey matter and women have more white matter), and secondary characteristics such as body fats distributions (including breasts) and bodily hair. Bio-medical research has consistently sought to link such differences to innate "personalities" or psychological explanations for perceived differences in behaviour and effective experiences. However, sociologists and socio-cultural anthropologists as well as many psychologists have tended rather to focus on the ways in which symbolic meaning and practices are associated with biological features of "sex" to "cultural construct of gender".

Since the nineties, theorists have drawn attention to the fact that the medical assignment of "sex" at birth is also a culturally constructed practice. Ruth Hubbard (1990), cites Anne Fausto-Sterling estimation that one-two per cent of babies are actually born with ambiguous sexual characteristics (chromosomal, gonad, and sex do not always corroborate with one another) and proposes the existence of at least five sexes. Like Judith Butler (1990), Hubbard sees the surgical procedures to "correct" the genitals of inter-sexes infants as an example of science being used to force upon "natural" bodies to conform to the cultural perceptions.

In response to the increasing abstraction of gender theory with everything being reduced to cultural constructions, Toril

Moi's essay, *What is a Woman* (2001), argues the need to abandon the "gender" concept altogether and return to a theory embedded within a material world. Her "lived body" concept proposes that a person's identity interaction with experience of their world is directly related to the materiality of his/her body, its physical attributes and capacities, the reactions it evokes from others, and its "situation" within a historically specific cultural environment. Moreover, the body's inhabitant has projects and goals, which determine the way a person interacts with this "situation". Thus, the limits of the "gender concept" tend to imply that people are subject to the roles imposed upon them by "culture" and transcended by the "lived body" theory. However, as Iris Marion Young (2005), points out in the essay "Lived Body versus Gender", such a conceptualisation is more useful to describe individual experience than macro-logical, social structure and their organisation. Young concludes that "gender" continues to be necessary in political and sociological approaches to gender relations.

Contribution of Anthropological Studies to Gender

Anthropological studies have highlighted cross-cultural variation in human behaviour, social structure and belief/ meaning systems, which in the early 20th century helped draw attention to the social and historical specificity of the Western notion of gender and denied their having an ontological or biological basis.

However, as have been argued by Henrietta Moore (1998), and other feminist anthropologists, male bias and gender blindness or ethno-centricism has been a marked feature of the formational stages of anthropology as a discipline. Moore remarks that women were observed, photographed and documented by anthropologists, but their opinions were generally not represented or even listened to.

She attributes this to the fact that majority of anthropologists up to the sixties or seventies and beyond were males. As such, they not only found it difficult to approach women (social context) but also tended to assume that men made better informants as they were likely to have political/ ritual power and knowledge, an assumption resulting from their knowledge of their own (Western) societies. Moore notes that even female ethnographers were likely to hold this view, since they had been educated within the male-dominated Western academic system. The impression that male informants were more "articulate" is understood as an indication that their statements/models of society were simply more intelligible (familiar) to social scientists.

The fundamental paradigm, which emerged and still continues to be very significant within the anthropological approach to the study of gender relations, is the study of kinship. This situates gender within the social structure, which has significant implications for power and economic relations. However, the relegation of women to mere symbols or commodities within structural systems reiterates a male world view in which women and their activities are considered to merely serve the purpose of men or social reproduction.

Margaret Mead (1935) drew attention to the process of socialisation and its influence on culturally different patterns of gendered behaviour and experience, including sexuality in the first half of the 20th century. But the social changes within Europe and America led women anthropologists in the sixties and seventies to investigate gender relations across cultures with a political imperative, especially in asking whether women's subordination was universal or a feature unique to capitalist society. Sherry Ortners' (1974: 67-88) complex reasoning that women are seen as "closer to nature" than men as a result of their association with children and the "domestic sphere" because of their reduced mobility enforced by lactation and pregnancy led her to conclude that this could explain their "devaluation" in most or all societies.

Rosaldo, however, in "*The Use and Abuse of Anthropology*" (1980: 389-417), proposed as Moore (1998) does in feminist anthropology that women and feminist anthropology should look to develop new lines of questioning rather than follow male paradigms of seeking to explain perceived "universals", or simply cataloguing women's experiences as examples of their subordinations. Such questions include the social, cultural and historical specificities of gender relations and the ways they are symbolically represented or articulated in practices.

Observation

In the traditional Zomi society, the father is the head of the family. He is mostly responsible for inter-clan and community relations in terms of authority and decision-making. By custom and convention, a Zomi woman had no inheritance rights or share in the property of her father. Women had no freedom to choose their future partner, which was entirely in the hands of their parents. The bias against women in Zomi customary laws is amply highlighted by the specific penalties prescribed for women, who committed adultery. But the question here is what happened to the man with whom she had committed the act of adultery? Zomi custom is completely silent on this.

Woman had been regarded as a property of man and some people take divorce very light. *"Daisia leh numei kikhek thei"* was the old saying, which means 'broken fencing and woman are liable to change'. A woman (wife) and old fencing can be replaced any time. If a husband is tired of his wife, he tells her to go and she returns to her father's house. In such a case, the husband cannot recover the bride price he paid. In case a wife leaves her husband on her own will, then her bride price is returned by her father. "If, however, the man has ill-treated his wife, she may leave him and he cannot claim the price he paid for her" (Carey and Tuck 1976: 210). In case, a husband dies without any issue, the wife returns to her father's house. In case, a wife dies without any issue or an issue, before paying bride price, before funeral takes place the bride price must be settled, otherwise, the wife's father has the right to claim the body of his daughter being unpaid for.

The issue of the marriage belongs to the father in case of separation or divorce and the mother has no claim to her children (*Ibid*). Divorce is permissible in case of barrenness as woman is supposed to be progenitor of children. No one could tell who is barren but the blame goes to the wife as no scientific investigation ever carried out in such a case. Though divorce becomes a possibility, the Zomis by nature are faithful and divorce is rare as a whole (Nang 2007). The socio-cultural system is, therefore, based on, and strengthened by, the values embodied in patriarchy, the traditional power structure that operates at the core of the Zomi society, i.e., the village. The traditional governing system of the Zomi has been the chieftainship. Only males have the right to chieftainship while memberships in village administration are on the basis of clan, which only males can represent. It can be argued that the perception that only males constitute the "public" is a logical outcome of the customary practices of female exclusion from traditional meetings and decision-making institutions.

However, in spite of the Zomi women being sidelined, deprived of many rights and marginalised by the traditional system, this does not mean that women in traditional Zomi society were just passive members. In fact, the whole social system starting from the household cannot be run or maintained without the active participation of the women. In agriculture practices, even womenfolk acts as the keeper of the seeds to be planted in the jhums. In the socialisation process, it is the women who are the keeper of tradition and impart traditional values and knowledge to the children within the household. Women also played important role in maintaining inter-clan relations and diffusing many volatile situations. Regardless of these, women in traditional Zomi patriarchal society are, more often than not, left unacknowledged, unsung and marginalised through socially induced perceptions of women maintained by the male-dominated society which could be perceived through the sayings like, "The wisdom of women does not extend beyond the banks of a river", "Let women and dogs bark as they like", "Women and crabs have no religion", etc.

Men are considered as the upholder of the family's tradition, while women are only temporary members of her natal family and establish her permanent status only after her marriage. Men are considered as the head of the family, clan and village. They are the representative of their respective units and, as such, they represent the decision-making body. As Zehol (2006: 99-10) noted, the husband takes all major decisions inside and outside the family. The wife may be consulted and may even indirectly influence her husband. The issue is that though patriarchies depend on their wives or mothers, yet they contrive to make the importance of motherhood invisible. Thus, gender asymmetry is visible in the light of men as the head in the family and society, who wield authority in their hands and women who follow the headship of their men.

The concept of what is feminine and what is considered as masculine seems to manifest itself in every aspect of their life. For instance, the structure of the society itself sanctions to men and women different status. Man is always given the title of a householder, while woman is only acknowledged in the society as daughter of the father or wife of her husband. A woman's dependent status itself shows asymmetrical relations based on gender, which is structured in different institutions of the society.

As descent is traced from the male line, women are not entitled to inherit any ancestral property. If a person does not have son, then the right to inherit goes to the next kin. In this light, the son preference becomes very apparent among the patrilineal society in order to uphold the tradition of the family. However, this does not mean that girls are not welcome in the family. The birth of a girl is always welcome in the family to help the parents, but not as upholder of the family's tradition. Thus, patriarchy seems to favour boys over girls for the said reason and it is a matter of family's pride and for security reasons to have someone of their own to inherit the name, line and ancestral property in terms of land, field and woodland.

Further, gender-based practices appear to be deeply rooted in the culture of the Zomi patrilineal societies as it is apparent in the taboos, folklores and sayings of the people which are passed down through oral tradition. Moreover, Zehol's (1998) account of gender relation in Naga patrilineal society draws attention to women in patrilineal society's economic dependence on men. British administrator, Steward, in his notes on "North Cachar" described the Zomis in this way, "the women appear more squat than the men even, but are strong and lusty, and quite as industrious and indefatigable as Naga women, working hard all day either at home or in the fields, and accustomed to carry heavy loads. The men, like the Nagas, are inclined to be lazy, though not to such an extent as that tribe" (Steward 1855: 582-701). Although women, especially in the rural villages, are often active in the production process and their activities are essential for the maintenance of economic continuity of their societies, they do not have the opportunity to accumulate wealth. Besides, the customary laws of the various Zomi tribes are clearly in favour of the men, who continue to subscribe to them in order to retain their superiority vis-à-vis the women in their own societies. The factors like education, occupation and religion do not seem to have had any success towards overcoming such gender bias among the men, though the women are not without such bias either.

As agents in the maintenance of tribe/community boundaries, however, Zehol (2009) argues that women's knowledge in the domestic realm regarding food practices and rituals (granary) or their preparation gives them a certain sense of power and prestige in their families. It is important to note that since women are economically dependent on their families, it is understandable that maintaining ritual purity and observing prescriptions of boundary maintenance become a prerogative for them. However, in terms of political empowerment, women in Zomi society are still not allowed to take part in the deliberations of the contemporary traditional village council. Such observations about women not playing leadership roles in political or socio-religious matters are, however, not peculiar of the tribal societies.

Today, Zomi women indeed have experienced significant improvement in lifestyle and opportunities but they have a long way to go before they achieve equity within their respective society. Some would want to dismiss this idea of gender equality or rather women's equality as a Western idea, which is a wrong assumption. In fact, in 1950, the Constitution of India put women and men on the same parameter. Unlike in Western democracies where men were granted the franchise well before women, in India's first general elections held in 1952, all citizens over the age of 18 were encouraged to vote, regardless of their class, caste or gender.

While modern education, democratisation and other development are gradually awakening a feminist consciousness amongst many Zomi women who are trying to work for meaningful change, the goal remains elusive in the face of patriarchal obstacles. Along with the educational, economic and other social attainments of the women, a concomitant social consciousness in the Zomi males regarding gender stereotypes is a prerequisite for gender equity. The state government can also help initiate positive changes in existing customary practices to traditional governance and the hereditary system.

Indeed, many are arguing for a strengthening or replication of traditional community institutions, paying little attention to the unequal social relations, especially unequal gender relations these institutions typically embody. Gender hierarchies and ideologies are not just in terms of norms and perceptions, but in terms of deeply embedded aspect relating in particular to (i) gender division of labour, (ii) property rights, and (iii) authority and access to public decision-making forums. As noted, the gender division of labour is the basis for women's having a double work burden. Women's lack of ownership in land increases their dependence. And, above all, due to their low representation in decision-making forums, they have little say in the rules governing themselves. Rendering these hierarchical structures historically invisibly also make invisible their continuation in the present context.

Conclusion

Gender has become an important category of social analysis and any contemporary discourse attracts the need to venture into the gender system of a given society. Thus, gender is not a simple notion in a cultural context. It forms rather a complex web of social action and relation forming a system in it. A wide scope lays ahead for scholars to relook at and redefine social realities through gender perspectives that can generate valuable and relevant database, which can be used for the practical benefit for humankind, in general, and women, in particular.

References

Beauvoir, Simone (1949): *The Second Sex* (Canada: Penguin Books Ltd.).

Butler, Judith (1990): *Gender Trouble: Feminism and the Subversion of Identity* (New York: Rutledge).

Carey, B.S. and H.N. Tuck (1976): *Chin Hills: A History of the People, Our Dealings with Them, Their Customs and Manners, and a Gazetteer of Their Country* (Aizawl, Mizoram: Tribal Research Institute), First print 1896.

Connell, R.W. (2002): *Gender* (Cambridge: Polity Press).

Hubbard, Ruth (1990): *The Politics of Women's Biology* (New Brunswick: Rutgers University Press).

Mead, M. (1935): *Sex and Temperament in Three Primitive Societies* (New York: Morrow).

Moi, Toril (2001): *What is a Woman?* (New York: Oxford University Press).

Moore, Henriett L. (1998): *Feminism and Anthropology* (Cambridge: Polity Press).

Nang, Gin Khan (2007): *Zomi Life and Culture* (Pasadena, CA 91104, USA: Fuller Theological Seminary).

Ortner, Sherry (1974): "Is Female to Male as Nature is to Culture?", in M Rosaldo and M. Lamphere (ed), *Woman, Culture and Society* (Stanford: Stanford University Press), 67-88.

Rosaldo, M.Z. (1980): "The Use and Abuse of Anthropology: Reflections on Feminism and Cross-cultural Understanding", *Signs: Journal of Women in Culture and Society* (Chicago: The University of Chicago Press), 5(3): 389-417.

Rubin, Gayle (1975): "The Traffic in Women: Notes on the Political Economy of Sex", in R.R. Reiter (ed.), *Towards an Anthropology of Women* (New York: Monthly Review Press), 157-210.

Steward, R. (1855): *Notes on North Cachar* (Calcutta: Journal, Asiatic Society of Bengal), 24: 582-701.

Young, Iris Marion (2005): "Lived Body versus Gender: Reflections on Social Structure and Subjectivity", in *On Female Body Experience: 'Throwing Like a Girl' and Other Essays* (Oxford University Press).

Zehol, L and Kevekha Kevin Zehol (2009): *The Legendary Naga Village—A Reader (Khezhakeno)* (Nagaland: Heritage Publishing House).

Zehol, Lucy (2006): "Gender Issues in the Tribal Society of North-East India: Some Observations", *Bulletin of the Department of Anthropology* (Assam: Dibrugarh University), 34:99-10.

Zehol, Lucy ed. (1998): *Women in Naga Society* (New Delhi: Regency Publications).

4

Gender Equality among the Zomis

Tara Manchin Hangzo

Introduction

The term gender equality generally implies equal treatment of boys and girls in all spheres of life unless there is a sound biological reason for different treatment. It can also refer to the social roles that men and women play and the power relation between them. Society has dictated distinctive roles for men and women by reserving traditional occupations and behaviour. Gender equity has to do with access to resources and opportunity for men and women, boys and girls. However, whether this concept has been realised among the Zomis of the North-East (NE) India is something to be explored.

History shows that the movement towards gender equality, especially in the Western countries, began with the suffragette movement of the late 19th century, which sought to allow women to vote and hold elected office. Since then much progress has been made in the Western countries. But the objective of gender equality has not been fully achieved worldwide, especially in the developing country like India, and it is a relatively new concept for the Zomi community.

In India, girls and women face a barrage of abuses largely due to the patriarchal attitudes of men. These include female foeticide, "honour" killings, acid attacks, rapes, trafficking and dowry murders. There were 228,650 reported crimes committed against women in 2011, an increase of seven per cent from the year 2010 (National Crimes Records Bureau 2011). According to Human Development Index (HDI) 2011 report, India ranked 129 out of 146 countries on the gender inequality index. There are many reported cases of violence against north-eastern women in India in the recent past. Zomis, being Indian and living in many parts of India, are not immune to such abuses/attacks.

Even United Nations (UN) bodies saw the need for empowerment of girls and women world-wide and so created *UN WOMEN—An Entity for Gender Equality and Empowerment of Women* that would lead the work on gender equality within the UN system. UN WOMEN was created by the UN General Assembly on 2nd July 2010 to accelerate progress in meeting the needs of women and girls worldwide.

Who are the Zomis?

The Zomis of the NE India are part of the 29 indigenous groups of people later known as Chin-Kuki-Lushais. In India, they can be defined as cloistered Scheduled Tribe communities that have governed themselves according to their own tribal customary laws for centuries. They are significantly and prominently found in the Chin Hills of Myanmar, in Manipur and Mizoram in India, in parts of Bangladesh, and even in south-east Asian countries.

Since the last century, significant progress has occurred among the Zomis. They have undergone what is "tantamount" to a complete change in the socio-economic and political sphere. This change can be attributed to the mass conversion to Christianity in the 19th century. Until the advent of Christianity, they were an agrarian society living off shift (jhum) cultivation and their social interactions were strictly traditional, following the tribal prescribed roles for men and women. The missionaries brought education and thereby introduced other forms of livelihood. The newly-educated Zomi men like pastors, teachers and soldiers were the potent force for changes in the Zomi society as they gained new perspective due to education and changed world view and exposure to the Western world like France and UK that awakened social, economic and political awareness. It is important to note that there was no woman chief, pastor, teacher, soldier then.

Although the Zomis have coexisted with the Hindu Meiteis in Manipur, they have for the most part preserved their social and cultural practices. What is interesting is that the introduction of a new religion, Christianity, has not made any significant impact on their traditional customs, such as the marriage and inheritance laws, folk songs and the institution of *"Indongta"*. *"Indongta"* is a family council. Every Zomi household has its own *"Indongta"*. When a son or brother separates from his parental home, an *"Indongta"* is instituted for him on the initiative of his father or elder brother. It is a formal organisation with recognised functions and customs related to marriage, bride price and the dissolution of marriage. The old traditional customs and taboos are still deeply rooted and entrenched in the community. In other words, the customary laws still prevail and continue to rule the social life of the people.

LET US SEE IF GENDER EQUALITY OR INEQUALITIES EXIST IN THE ZOMI SOCIETY

The Status of Zomi Women

The social structures of the Zomis are constructed/ designed in such a way that the status of woman to man in the society is equal but her many rights are curbed rendering her to a lower level to man. Women's role in the economic and family areas are recognised and accepted as norms. But in the tradition, rituals and political affairs are reserved for men. Society still considers them as subordinate and unreliable in important decision-making process outside the domain of the house.

What is paradoxical is that the rights of women are different inside and outside the home. While she could rule as queen in her own household, she has no voice outside. They are involved in decision-making of important family matters such as negotiating marriages, improvement and construction of a house, matters relating to children's education and health care.

This is because of the patriarchal set-up, customary laws and traditional beliefs that are still governing the society. Woman is considered as a helper to man, as "Eve" was to "Adam", and her full membership to the family she marries into is completed once she bore a male child to continue the family linage. Derogatory remarks about the wisdom of women's opinion not being worth its salt are still being practised and their worth is still not recognised.

In the days of yore because of the isolation from the mainstream plain people for many years, it was assumed that the status of Zomi women was relatively high because of the absence of the gender discrimination (as they toil side by side in the fields). However, Zomi's exposure and assimilation to mainstream Hindu culture and tradition have led to some evidence of gender discrimination and disparity in their customary practices.

Zomi women enjoy considerable freedom when it comes to choosing their life partners. They are never forced to marry against their will. Generally, compared to the Hindu women, the Zomi tribal women have enjoyed greater freedom and higher status. However, she has no voice on policy change, village affairs, whether she could stand for election, hold important autonomous council membership, or become a pastor, to quote a few examples.

Marriage Customs among the Zomis

Zomis follow agamous marriage in which a man could marry any woman within and outside Zomi clan. They follow agamy. The custom of paying *"manpi"*, a bride price, is prevalent, a prerequisite to a Zomi marriage. It is not dowry, as the people involved in the marriage negotiation do it to safeguard the bride's welfare and interests. In other words, it could be an indication of the high social value that men placed on their bride to be. In earlier times, bride price had to be earned by young men. The principal price *"sial"* (mithuns) was the accepted bride price in the olden days. Therefore, the fairer the maiden, the higher is the number of mithuns that must be paid. But in modern time, the bride price is a fixed amount equal for all. There is slight variation in the amount among the different Zomi tribes. For instance, rupees 3,000 for Paite and rupees 420 for Mizos.

"Manpi" is paid by the bridegroom side to the bride's parents and has to be received by the father of the bride. In case of abandonment or divorce, the mother of the bride is forbidden to receive the bride price. In the case of a deceased father, the bride price goes to the nearest male relative on the father's side, preferably to the uncle or the male member who is the heir apparent. The settlement of paying the bride price must be completed before a marriage could be solemnised in the Church of the bridegroom. In the case of a single parent household headed by a mother, the uncles of the bride and the *"Indongta"* decide all aspects while the women are relegated to serve tea and remained as spectators. Even if the mother or other women were asked for their opinion, they will answer that they agree with whatever have been decided by the *"Indongta"*.

Qualities of a Bride

The ideal Zomi bride must have these attributes—involved in Church activities, modest, chaste, respectful and faithful rather than just beauty, education or wealth. In earlier times, her skills at farming and weaving were also considered. Young women take active part in Church activities, sing in the choir and make themselves more visible. A modern Zomi woman clearly models her behaviour according to Christian values as her spiritual life is one of the criteria for a good wife. But as for a man, the criteria cannot be decided by the woman. She has to accept him as he is if she loves him.

There are marked differences between the Zomi women and the mainstream Hindu women where beauty and material success is the desired qualities of the bride-to-be. The practices of dowry, child marriage and bride burning are unknown in Zomi society. Zomi women do not have to face the indignity of advertising for a bridegroom in the local newspapers and have scores of men reject and humiliate her before she finds her life partner. Girls are at a liberty to choose their own life partners. There is no age bar or a pressure applied for a Zomi woman to marry at a certain age. The mean age of marriage for tribal women is higher than the mean age of marriage for Hindu women.

Child marriage was prevalent among the Hindus, as parents wanted their daughters to marry early to preserve their virginity and purity. However, such stigma did not exist for the Zomi women who were indifferent to the notions of purity and pollution. What is notable in the 21st century is the trend of marrying outside the Zomi clan, and marrying foreigners is more prevalent among the girls than boys. This is an indicator of the freedom given to girls and the non-discriminatory attitude of the community towards outsiders.

Courtship

The Zomi way of courtship in older days when the main occupation was agriculture is unique. The courtship practised is known as *"in sung kihel"* (in-house) where suitors could call on young woman at her home and interact under the chaperone of the parents. About six to seven suitors could call upon the girl they fancy at her house after sundown and chit-chat, smoke while she works on her loom. Great restraint is shown by the boys to behave in such a manner that decorum of the house is maintained. The girl discloses her preference by various means like giving him a full/half cup of tea, or ties a certain coloured thread around the cigarette to indicate her availability reciprocity. Due to changes in livelihood and move to urban areas, courtship among the Zomis has followed mainstream dating habits, though young men continue to visit homes and interact with the family.

Addressing the Husband

A Zomi woman after her marriage has to address her husband not by name but affix the terms *"U"* to her husband's name like, UPau, Uthang, etc. After the children arrive, they address their husband with the child's name and affix *"pa"*, meaning father, such that he becomes known as the child's father. For example *"Minlian pa"* means father of Minlian. This is a practice demanded by customary law for the wife to show respect and submission to the husband. It is still practised in present times and unlikely to change. Zomi women automatically assume the husband's surname upon marriage.

In lieu of dowry, Zomi girls must carry few essential items upon marriage called *"thuam"*. The *"thuam"* (stuffs) she carries at the time of marriage is not dowry in the real sense. This consists of the traditional shawl to cover the body of her husband in case of his death, *"puanteng"* (wrap around), women box, *"puanpi"* (cotton quilt), hoe, space, axe, beaded necklace, tuibuk pipe, loom, bamboo baskets, etc. Nowadays, depending on the economic status of the girl, her *"thuam"* size has increased manifold. The rich Zomi girls now carry goods that could rival the Hindu dowry.

Widow Remarriage

Remarriage for widows/widowers is accepted by the society. However, the number of widower remarriage is higher than that of the widows as a direct result of tribal laws. A widower by virtue of tribal laws has full right to his property, custody of his children as well as a right to a new alliance after a year of mourning. However, for a widow, remarriage entails giving up her rights to her young children, which a mother is not willing to do. As a result, widows often choose to remain single rather than sacrifice her children.

A widower can marry a much young girl and have children but older woman marrying a much younger man is looked upon with askance and not accepted by the society. The high rate of death of many young men in the eighties and nineties due to drug overdose, HIV/AIDS/alcohol and insurgency had created many widows in their 20s who never remarried. The few who remarried often had failed marriages. What is preventing young widows from remarriage is something that the community needs to explore. It is important that widows are not stigmatised by the society and should be allowed to lead a normal life.

Son as a Continuation of the Clan

Zomi society is still patriarchal where complete authority is vested in the male. As such, bearing a son is mandatory for a married woman to ensure that *"min phung luah ding"* (the surname of the husband) continues to the next generation. In the past, this was easily achieved as large family structure was the norm and family planning was rare. A married woman, who bore ten children, was sure to produce at least one son amongst the ten. However, with modern cost and constraints in child rising, Zomis in the metro areas tend to have fewer children and bearing a son to ensure *"min phung luah ding"* and *"beh phung"* will continue to become a challenge among them. *"Beh phung"* system is derived from the concept that *"beh"* (clan) relationship is maintained through sons and not daughters. The lineage is counted from the first son who is the inheritor of the property of the parents.

When it comes to naming the new-born child, Zomi cannot simply choose names according to whim and fancy. In a society that is patrilineal, the eldest son of the eldest male member is compulsorily named after the last syllable of the paternal grandfather. In an average family size of four to five children, the aunts and uncles have the privilege of giving part of their names and thereby serve as godparents to the child. Zomis put strong emphasis on taking the names of their ancestors. Some modern families affix a Christian name like Michael, but it is still an honour to have a Zomi name as it shows your lineage and ancestry.

Divorce Laws of the Zomis

Divorce is permissible in the society and not frown upon, but also not encouraged among the Zomis. As they are Christians, marriage is considered a sacred bond, inseparable, except by an event of death. Decision for divorce is taken very seriously and carried out only in agreement with *"Indongta"* for valid reasons such as adultery, mental illness, barrenness and childlessness. Divorces occur but it is often the women who are blamed for failed marriages, while the men get away scot-free to pursue new alliances. There are many instances of remarriages where step-children go astray due to neglect.

Man or woman can initiate the divorce proceeding, if they so wish. According to the customary law, when the man divorces his wife, he has to return her bride price, and in case a wife leaves her husband voluntarily, then her father must return the bride price. Then, father or eldest brother in the family has the sole rights over the divorced daughter on family issues pertaining to her and they decide on her behalf.

Divorcee is not stigmatised or discriminated against but her rights are denied. Divorced women are denied custody of her children and have no right over the family property. She is entitled to take back only customary *"thuam"* if her husband divorces her. She will go completely empty-handed if she commits adultery. No financial support is ever extended to divorced spouses. There is no customary law that a man provides adequate maintenance for her welfare until she remarries. A recent case has emerged where the ex-husband provides maintenance for the ex-wife, but the practice is generally frowned upon. It is just a topic for gossip among bored housewives.

Most modern marriages are love marriages solemnised by the Church with the consent of the family, independent of the family courts. The family in consultation with the *"Indongta"* members will make the decisions. Mizoram is taking a lead in trying to bring about an ordinance over the customary divorce laws under the Mizo Hmeichhe Insuihkhawm Pawl

(Mizo women association), which have been fighting for the amendment of the customary laws for the past 40 years. Among the Mizos, a man can divorce his wife just by saying the word, "I divorce you" much like the Muslim's *"talaak"*. Among the other Zomi clans, divorce is more complex. The challenge is how the women of the other Zomi clans will follow Mizoram's example and start taking initiative to bring about a change in their own divorce customary laws and make it more women-friendly keeping in view their economic independence.

In the Zomi society, young girls are given the freedom to mingle with young men before marriage. The problem of having a child out of wedlock is a common phenomenon. The relatively easy Zomi custom that allows for the abhorrent practice of not accepting the pregnant girl or the child for various reasons is a social evil. According to their customary law, all the boy's family has to do is to send the *"Indongta"* members with meat as peace offering, pay a fine, the amount decided upon negotiation and the matter is settled. The *"Indongta"* makes the decision whether to accept the child at birth or after three years without the consent of the girl concerned. As a result, children are often raised by grandparents, or extended family members while the father or mother assumes the role of a sibling. Society does not stigmatise them and these children are brought up normally but the men have no role in their lives. Men are not made accountable for their misdeeds and many children grow up not knowing their fathers.

Inheritance Laws of the Zomis

According to the Zomi inheritance law, inheriting the property of parents is not simply inheriting properties but taking on the responsibility to care, to support parents and maintain the family. By tribal custom and laws, this responsibility rests only with the sons of the family. The first son will live in the family as inheritor and other sons will be separated after marriage, called *"inntuan"* (setting up of a new family). This law of inheritance has been revised by the Zomi Council (ZC) recently to accommodate women in special circumstances. But, whether they are put into practice or not is yet to be seen. There have been substantial changes to women's property rights, particularly in relation to their marital status. In the instance of a single progeny who is a woman, even after marriage she and her children would have the rights to her father's property. Otherwise, the only occasion a woman could get some of her father's property is during her marriage ceremony where she is given *"thuam"*.

In this modern age, Zomi girls are given rights to paddy field, house and land, besides modern gadgets, cars, etc., by well-to-do families. This dowry type of giving is normally not practised by Zomis. The girl received many household gifts at her send-off ceremony from the community. Some families have written wills or legal papers of the distribution of properties among brothers and sisters, but most just follow the tribal customary laws.

Some bias and gender depreciation still exist in their society as divorcees and widows are denied a share in the husband's property. In the case of a widow with minor children, a male relative, usually the brother of the deceased, takes charge of the property until the children come of age. A childless widow has no share in her deceased husband's property as the rights get transferred to the nearest nephews or uncles.

"Zu" Culture of the Zomi

Traditionally, *"zu"*, rice brewed wine, plays an important role as it was placed in the centre of social and religious activities, either in marriage, feast, festival and funeral. Women brew *"zu"* that was drunk and enjoyed by the whole family. Missionaries like EH East have remarked that Chins (Zomis) are the most drunken people he had come in contact with. Every occasion whether it is a joy or sorrow, they must drink and when drunk must dance.

The evil manifestation of drinking *"zu"* was felt in the violent crimes committed during drinking bouts. Embracing

Christianity has not led to discarding the drinking habits among the Zomis, though today, tea replaces the place of *"zu"* in ceremonies and rituals during marriages and festivals. The impact of their ancestors' drinking bouts is still to be seen in their quick embrace of new intoxicants like drug such as heroin No. 4, ganja and other pharmaceutical drugs.

Another accepted social custom is the consumption of tobacco products. There is no gender disparity when it comes to consumption of tobacco juice known as *"tuibuk"*. *"Tuibuk"* is enriched nicotine water shared by both men and women of the household. Visitors are offered *"tuibuk"* as a social gesture of welcome and it is the responsibility of the women to ensure that there is a continuous supply of it. Therefore, they constantly drag and puff at the smoke pipe to generate more of it.

Earlier, *"zu"* was prevalent. Now, the evils of drugs and alcohols such as the modern booze like whiskey, beer, vodka, rum, etc., have become rampant, especially among the youth. Drugs and drinking have turned men into demons and domestic violence has become rampant. Addicts often beat their wives and infect them with HIV, which pushed many widows into sex workers to survive. Gender-based domestic violence like harassing mothers and wives for money for drugs is unfortunately not considered a crime but seen as a problem within the family.

Drugs and the Zomis

Churachandpur, the biggest Zomi township in Manipur, has the largest number of Injecting Drug Users (IDU) of both male and female. When it comes to medical or other facilities, male IDUs have men-friendly clinics, hospitals and NGOs catering to their needs. Female IDUs are further stigmatised as many of them are forced into sex work to support their injecting and drinking habits. Parents often support the boys unwillingly out of their meagre salaries. Many of these young addicts choose to marry and when they die, the parents take on the responsibility of raising the orphans (the grand-children) while the mother, if young is expected to leave the marital home after the funeral concludes. The economic and the social impact of substance abuse is greatly felt by the Zomi community with terrible repercussions as almost each household has a story to tell about an addict son or daughter. Many young people, especially women, move into sex work and drugs to escape poverty and unemployment.

The Impact of Violence on Women

The continuing unrest and the armed conflicts have its impact on the Zomi society. Once a cloistered, compassionate society, we now see social evils like rape, domestic violence, HIV/AIDS. The armed conflict situation prevalent in North-East has intensified the violence faced by women in the form of sexual, mental or physical abuse, killings and clashes of women for no apparent reason. Although all the members of community are affected by the armed conflict, the impact on women and girls is far greater because of their vulnerability, their sex and status in the society. Zomi women are not immune to this assault. The region, under the shadow of conflict, has witnessed a resurgence of patriarchal values and norms, which have imposed some restrictions on the movement and behaviour of women. Most cases of sexual violence in the hills and valley of Manipur resulting from the armed conflict involved the armed forces and the Meitei insurgents. The Armed Forces (Special Power) Act 1958 has intimidated our menfolk rendering them helpless.

There are no helpline for women in distress, no mental hospital or shelter. The mentally unstable women are either kept at home locked in or are made to roam around freely as easy prey to social deviants. The government has no policies for gender sensitive matters. The big challenge for Zomi women will be how to initiate such activities and campaign for gender sensitive laws and have better facilities for women.

DOES GENDER EQUITY EXIST AMONG THE ZOMI SOCIETY?

Gender equity refers to the equal distribution of opportunities, of access to resources and of decision-making power between men and women in a society.

Education/Jobs

Changes to attitude to equality in education opportunities for Zomi boys and girls have undergone a cultural shift. Both the genders are seen competing for the same post like in management schools, engineering, civil services and medicine. Hence, many wife-husband relationships are moving towards equality because of education after the establishment of an English medium education in the early fifties. Access to modern education led to the social and economic empowerment of Zomi women in the secular sphere and job markets after acquiring degrees and diplomas. Zomi women joined the work force as nurses, teachers, doctors, bank officers, etc. Still the number of men working far productively exceeds that of women.

Labour

Zomi women in general have higher labour participation in comparison to the women of the non-tribal groups. Micro-enterprises are run by the women, which has enhanced their economic empowerment and benefits the whole family, especially the children. But the fact remains that most Zomi women in the informal sector (activities street vendors and small crafts workers) tend to remain in poverty since most informal services are survivalist and low income in nature. Unfortunately, greater labour force participation does not lead to greater female autonomy in the household.

Health

The apathy of the state government in the Zomi region has reduced several primary health centres and the community health centres in the hill areas to a non-functional state and are in a derelict condition with hardly doctors or nurses attending them. This has led to the breakdown of existing health services in the Zomi inhabited region. While the absence of doctors affected everybody, it is women who suffer most being unable to access health-care services in neighbouring towns or villages in absence of transport and the long distances. Therefore, maternal mortality amongst the Zomi women in remote hill areas is quite high as compared to their valley counterparts where better facilities exist.

Sex Ratio is a Key Indicator to Gauge Gender Equality

The clearest indicator of discrimination against women in India, as in most states, is the skewed sex ratio. Fortunately, for the Zomis and for the state of Manipur, the sex ratio is far from being skewed. According to the Census of India 2011, for the district of Churachandpur, the sex ratio in the age group of 0-6 shows an almost equal ratio of 0.65 per cent for a male child and for female child at 0.62 per cent (Census 2011). This is an indication of less gender discrimination and better care and treatment of female infants. While the number of girls to every 1,000 boys in India is declining at an alarming rate, this does not apply to the Zomis. There is an inherent fear that more numbers of girls will lead to many abuses and harassment.

Equity among Men and Women in Perception

Traditional Zomi society is based on patriarchal norms where complete authority is vested in a male. Men continue to exercise greater power as they are employed and are the bread earners for the family. Analysis shows that the cycle of power relations connects work and family. The higher the husband's occupational status, the greater are his powers and his participation in the kitchen would be zero. Many Zomi men prefer their wives to be non-working mothers, if they could afford it. The biggest challenge of a Zomi woman today is to balance working outside the home and taking care of housework. Domestic work and household chores are the sole prerogatives of the Zomi women. Men, whether employed or not, refuse to help in housework for fear of being termed as *"thaibawi"* (in English it can mean henpecked) by the people in the neighbourhood. In urban areas, a few men have started to help their wives with household chores and child-care, especially when both are working professionals.

Among the Zomis, the occupations of nursing, cleaning and child-care are considered to be women's work. The traditional division of work between the men and women is still in existence. Zomi women do not depend on maid-servant or helper unless in dire strait, so end up doing the household chores themselves. Often times, the wife pursues her career after marriage and following childbirth due to economic constraints and to make two ends meet in metro city where the cost of living is higher.

Gender divide and work demarcation began from *"Zawlbuk"* days. That is, young men's dormitory, an exclusive privilege where they received training in life skill education preparing them for manhood and life. Women and girls are forbidden to participate in the macho activities of the *"Zawlbuk"* such as wrestling, hunting, village administration, etc. *"Zawlbuk"* is now replaced by philanthropic organisations like Young Paite Association (YPA), Young Mizo Association (YMA) and one noteworthy activity is digging the graves for burial.

The girls were kept under the guidance of the mothers who imparted traditional skills of weaving, pottery and other household skills. Most Zomi women are weavers. They take great pride in the colourful and flowery clothes they spin and weave. The beautiful *"puans"* (clothes) they weave go to supplement their household income and to cater to the customs that demands the *"Puandum"* (a sacred cloth of the Zomis) to be utilised for social occasions. The *"Puandum"* still plays a significant role during funeral rites and marriages. It is customary to give *"Puandum"* to the bereaved family as a sign of respect to cover the body of the deceased and it is an integral part of the bride's *"moutam"*, or gifts for husband's family. In ancient times, Zomi women were expected to cover the funeral coffin of her husband with *"Puandum"* as a sign of chastity.

Literacy Rate and Women at Workplace

The literacy rate among the Zomi men and women is almost at par according to the Census of 2011 for Churachandpur district. Literacy rate for male at 88.34 per cent and female at 80.13 per cent have led to many young women seeking jobs in the government and private sectors. However, due to the scarcity of jobs in Manipur, combined with the mandatory bribes in lakhs (in hundred thousands) of rupees for each government job, men are given the preference for jobs in the family forcing the women to move to big cities. Many take jobs at call centres, working the graveyard shifts, thereby making them easy targets for sexual harassment and discrimination. For example, the largest number of nurses in Delhi comes from amongst the Zomi clans. Historically, women had lower levels of education than men did, but recently this trend seems to have begun to reverse.

Role of Christianity and its Impact on the Women

Christianity did not make much impact on women's role in the Church as the Zomi Church still functions in a traditionally male-dominated manner. Zomi society still staunchly maintains its old patriarchal structure in the Church sphere and only men rule over its activities. Some tribal customs have been accommodated to suit men's need to assert their authority such as the practice of using *"khuang"* (drum) solely for men's use during singing songs and in the formation of the local Church committee which consists of only male members of the Church.

The male pastor has replaced the traditional *"siampu"* (priest). The Church hierarchy still excludes women from any position of authority and ordained offices like that of "ministers" or *"elders"*. All the pastors are men and the preachings are conducted by men, while women are rarely given such an opportunity. Though a number of women are studying theology since the eighties, none has been ordained as a pastor yet.

Women are seated separately from the men in the Church. Though this is not considered gender discrimination, the traditional practice continues. Women and girls are expected to dress demurely and wear traditional *"puan"* (attire) or long skirt in the Church till today as part of dress code imposed on them. Women are assigned the role of teaching Sunday school. The Dorcas Society was formed exclusively for women where they are encouraged in fund raising projects. They have made excellent contributions through *"antang pham"* (handful of rice collection from every household) and *"talent hih pung"* (profitable micro-investment). The funds collected are seldom invested in Church projects that benefit women as a specific group. Given the inequality of opportunities for men and women, this resource allocation is questionable. The Zomi women are still locked out of the "sacred" sphere of the Church on gender basis. They are made to play a subordinate role and are not assertive enough to demand their rights to play a more active role in the Church sphere yet.

Women's Leadership Role in Political Arena

Are the Zomi women ready to join politics? My answer would be, "yes", provided an opportunity is given to them. It is a fact that there is inadequate representation of Zomi women in decision-making bodies. This is a fault of the design of their societal structure where the administration structure is dependent on the concept of male chieftainship with zero participation of women in the past which inadvertently reinforces the marginalisation of women.

In the present century, Zomi women have contested the state assembly and parliamentary elections and some got elected, though the actual contribution made by them is yet to be seen. Taking the case of Manipur, in the 1998 parliamentary election, Kim Gangte was elected but was defeated in the next round before she could make significant changes. In the state assembly in 2011, there was only one lady member from the hills and only one woman member in Autonomous District Council. Their contributions are yet to be seen. It is worth mentioning that the names of Zomi women who have contested the assembly elections in the past could be counted by hand since they are so few in number.

Zomi women are still struggling to break the shackles of patriarchal governance that has divided the role of women in the private and public spheres. The challenge now is to organise women as a change agent to bring about a political evolution. The biggest reason for non-participation of Zomi women in the village administration and in the political arena is because of the continued practices of customary laws of tribal society. If women do not play roles in village administrations, the leap to larger units is that much harder.

Other impediments could be lack of finance, self-confidence, family support, lack of awareness, the general patriarchy and criminalisation of politics at all levels. In other words, the environment is not yet conducive and women-friendly—without the support of the entire community and money power to jump into the fray—to be elected. The 30 per cent reservation for women has no meaning for Zomi women unless and until it is put into practice. The *"Nupi Lan"* of 1904 and 1939, the *"Meira Paibi Movement"* of the seventies and eighties or the systems like the Meitei Women *"Paja"* courts are unknown among the Zomi society. The Zomi Mothers' Association is still not at par with the *"Meira Paibis"* in terms of the power they yield.

Conclusion

Despite advances in education, a gendered approach to social, economic and political issues will continue to be a challenge among the Zomis. Lack of women's participation in the political sphere needs to be addressed to make their participation more meaningful and integral to the process of development for the society. Even the literate and educated in the higher strata of Zomi society are not totally free of the partisan view till date. Zomi society is still deeply entrenched in this traditional patriarchal set-up. Sexist attitudes and perception still mould and shape the thinking of the male. The only solution is reformation of age-old customs and traditions as a panacea for women's true empowerment and making Zomi women more proactive and assertive to bring about a change in policies related to gender equality. It is high time women play a larger role, be it in the social and political spheres.

In North-East India context with entrenched gender inequalities and armed conflicts, women are deeply affected. All kinds of violence against women and/or gender bias against them have to stop if any progress is to be seen in the society.

References

2008: "Mizo divorce law soon to prevent *talaaq* equivalent's misuse", *The Indian Express*, Aizawl, 11th November.

Behal, Monisha (2004): *Violence against Women in North-East India: An Enquiry*, The North-East Network.

Census of India 2011.

Hauzel, Kamkhenthang (1977): *Household Council or Inndongta among the Paite of Lungchin*, Manipur South District.

Kamkhenthang, H (1986): "Groping for Identity", in H Kamkhenthang, S Prim Vaiphei, et. al. (ed.), *In Search of Identity* (Imphal: Kuki-Chin Baptist Union), 1-16.

Maharana, A (1998): *On Tribal Fertility in the late 19th Century India*, Working paper Series No. 98.01 (Harvard Centre for Population and Development Studies, Harvard University).

Mitra, A (2007): "The Status of Women among the Scheduled Tribes in India", *The Journal of Socio-economics*, DOi 10.1016/jsocec. 2006.212.077.

Nang, Gin Khan (2007): *Zomi Life and Culture* (Pasadena, CA: Fuller Theological Seminary).

5

A Gender Perspective on Democratisation

Ninglun Hanghal

This paper contains my thoughts as a woman, belonging to the Paite community, one of the ethnic groups of the Zomi, and who grew up in Lamka, Churachandpur district of Manipur. Moreover, as someone who writes about women of North-East (NE) India, my thoughts are based on self-experiences, understanding and interactions with women leaders. The subject is personal and that obviously is political.

When I filled up my matriculation examination form, I did not include my surname (the family/clan name). Therefore, all my educational certificates from matriculation to master's degree, have no second name. Perhaps, it was not required or nobody felt the need at that point of time, neither was I advised by the institution nor my family. Moreover, I kept on hearing in the family and in the social interactions a very popular saying, "Women have no (permanent) clan". Perhaps that was one key factor. This is not a law but the fact that it is an accepted norm that a woman takes her father's surname before marriage and her husband's surname after marriage.

Today, it is necessary to mention the first name; and the second name has also become a necessity. And for the Zomis, mostly amongst the educated, the need to include surnames for official or educational purpose has arisen and become important as well. Therefore, we see women changing names under legal procedures and published in the newspapers.

Change in names indicates marital status, automatically changing the women's status from a Miss to Mrs. If one observe an introduction of a Zomi woman, particularly in social gatherings, it goes like this. "My name is Ching", followed by "I am the wife of Mr. x, y...".

In the early eighties, I visited Phaitong, my paternal village in Thanlon sub-division in Churachandpur district. Early morning, I heard a thumping sound of a "thud, thud...". By the time I got up, the sound was no more and nobody was around in the house except my grandfather (mother's father) who was no longer strong enough to go to the *jhum* (cultivation field). I could see children around but no adults, except old men, women or the sick or disabled. Later, I realised that the sound was the manual pounding, a de-husking of paddy by the women folk for daily consumption. The daily life of the women folk in every household would begin by fetching water from the spring/river. They would carry a basket full of water filled in a set of about 10-15 bamboo trunk in about four feet length. Then, they would come back and pound the paddy for the day or sometimes for more days, cook, serve it and left for the *jhum* field.

Cultivation and production for consumption in the Zomi society is a collective effort of men and women. While men mostly take up work that require more physical strength such as clearing and preparing the *jhum*; for women their role involved from the beginning to the end till the harvest. In off-season, that is mostly post-harvest till the next *jhum* cycle, women are engaged in works such as weaving cloths, besides the non-stop domestic chores.

My mother would tell us, more like a tale, when she was still too young to go to the *jhum*, she looked after her younger siblings (she was the third among seven children). She would attend the government primary school with her siblings in tow. My mother told us that all her brothers were away from home for higher education. When she became a little older (after finishing the primary class and of course when her younger siblings no longer need her care), she began the *jhum* work, followed by roles and responsibilities prescribed for women.

Fortunately, for me, probably due to the changing time, I enjoyed the same privileges as my brothers as far as education is concerned. But it may be mentioned here that for girls there is no compromising on the domestic chores. Simultaneously, studying, cooking, washing, cleaning and other helping hand required of us in the kitchen and in social "dos" such as in case of death, social functions, etc.

I grew up under constant reminder of "dos" and "don'ts". In any matters when asked for permission like going to a movie, or outing/picnic, etc., the reply would be *"numei mei"*, meaning to say, you are a woman so don't even think about it. *"Numei"*, a combination of two words, *"nu"* and *"mei"*, literally mean "female" and "maid" (female maid). In Mizo, it is even worst, for the term they use for female is *"hmeichhia"*, which literally means an ugly maid, where *"hmei"* stands for maid and *"chhia"* means ugly.

In private (at homes), the girls are required to respect family members, and not to fight; while in public, they should keep in mind, "don't laugh too loud", "decent dressing", "you should not touch/hug or fight with boys/men". And if one gets into a problem, fights, accident, or extreme case such as assault, the common comments and/or remarks that follow are *"numei mei"*, why did you go there? Why did you do that? You should have known this! There is no argument; you are on the wrong side.

There are characters and behaviours for girls that would categorise them good and bad girls. Good girls go to Church, obey parents, elders, men, etc. For those who dare to go out of the way, would be categorised as "bad girls", or were stigmatised, especially if one is divorcee, a single mother or an unmarried mother. There are also instances of "social ostracism" of a woman who does not respect "social norms". Social norms basically are social behaviours prescribed and dictated by the elders/leaders. Case in point, a woman marrying outside the community, or a woman selling liquor or a woman caught in "adultery".

It felt like mourning a death when my sisters got married. We have a *"khakna"* ceremony, literally meaning, "send off". A woman when married is no longer part of the family. Therefore, the traditional ceremony or customary feast and rituals were actually a "farewell".

On the economic front, many Zomi women are today employed in offices. They work as teachers and other professional jobs. More women are seen in jobs in the urban commercial centres such as in Lamka (headquarter town of Churachandpur district, Manipur). Main market in old and new *bazaar* and recently the Tuibuang bazaar, are mostly (more than three-fourth) run and managed by women vendors. Moreover, shopkeepers, hoteliers along the Teddim and Tipaimukh road were mostly women. Also today, we see many women working in metro cities across India, in various private and public sectors.

It is a fact that in a society like the Zomis, selling vegetables or related items is regarded as an extension of the kitchen, perceived as a woman's place and her role in providing food to the family. While clothes and clothing stores, shops are yet another perceived extension of "weaving" and handloom works, historically and since generations was the job of a woman.

On a mere assumption, it appears that Zomi women did hold the economy in terms of earning and production. On a closer observation, they were actually the "workers", the labour force. As a labour force, Zomi women, and North-East women at large, face tremendous vulnerability, particularly in metro cities, especially those working in graveyard shifts and hospitality sectors. NE women at large and Zomi women in specific were the main bread-earners of the family. As much as women were perceived to be bearers of identity of community/tribe/groups, they become the site of racial attacks and abuse. Further, it is sad to note that women victims were stigmatised by their own community. It may be mentioned that in the infamous Delhi's Dhaula Kuan rape case of North-East woman in 2005, the victim was "packed off" to her home state by the community leaders.

Women involved in activities, such as protest against rape, political rallies and demonstrations, would be known as "activist" with an underlining tone. This includes me as well. When cases such as attacks on NE women in Delhi were reported, the first question people, NE people in specific, would ask was which community? Which tribe? This would be followed by comments such as "she deserves it", "our women are too open" and other derogatory remarks.

There are women organisations such as the Zomi Mothers' Association (ZMA) which have done tremendous philanthropic and welfare services. It may be underlined that the ZMA was formed in the aftermath of the 1997 clash between the Zomis and the Kukis. Thus, the mothers were mainly picking up the pieces of the post violence. Their roles and responsibilities were merely limited to care and support of the victims. As of today, they continue to do so.

In terms of Zomi women's participation in political space, it is almost nil. There is only one woman member of Autonomous District Council (ADC), named Grace Zamnu, in 2013 out of a total of 26 (2 nominated) in Churachandpur ADC. There is no Zomi woman state legislative member. Moreover, it is pertinent to note that Zomi women rarely, in exceptional cases of one or two, contested in the electoral politics. Further, it may be mentioned that in the overall six district councils in Manipur, there are 136 members, out of which there are only five women. In the 60-member legislative assembly of Manipur, there are only three women elected members—two in the Valley and one in the tribal hill districts.

Though there are constitutional provisions and other democratic processes such as The Manipur (Hill Areas) Autonomous District Council Act 1971, the traditional institutions and customary practices still override the secular and modern systems.

The Paite Customary Law Commission in its *"Pulakna"* (introduction) in the recently documented *Paite Customary Law, Paite Pupa Ngeina Dan* (2nd amendment, 2013) stated that traditions and customary laws draw more attachment and respect from the people. The introduction also noted that regulation such as Manipur Hills Regulation 1947 does not in any way elevate nor better the existing customary laws. In its first publication, the then President of the Paite National Council (now Paite Tribe Council), in his foreword underlined the need for a written oral customary laws that have been used since generations. And that The Indian Penal Code (IPC) cannot be implemented fully in a society like the Paites (or the indigenous self ruled people at large).

Beside others, here is a look at some of the key Paite customary laws concerning women.

Bride price fixed at rupees 3,000 an equivalent of an adult mithun and a calf. Originally, bride price and *"thaman"*, that is, price of body and soul was based on the belief "transfer of soul" and that a payment was made to "soul spirit" that her husband is officially permitted to bury his wife on her death.

Payment of bride price is not selling a woman, but a physical transference of the bride from her natal family (Kamkhenthang 2002). A symbolic gesture, but over the years this has been used and misused as a means to belittle or harassed women. Moreover, with monetary involvement, eventually the bride price evolved or rather transformed more or less like a "monetary transaction".

In case of a divorce by her husband, a woman can retain her "price" or the *"mou vanken"*. *"Mou vanken"* is the gifts she receives at the time of the marriage, but cannot claim it back in case she is the one who wants to leave her husband. In whatever circumstance or situation, she cannot claim her children. We do not hear or know of any maintenance after divorce for a Paite woman, who was/is a dependent on her husband in terms of economy.

In her book, *Women's Status in North-Eastern India,* Sindhu Phadke wrote, "The practice of bride price in a majority of North-East societies is indicative of a girl being viewed as an asset for her parental family. The groom and his family therefore try to compensate for the loss to the bride's family by giving bride price whether in the form of money, a feast for the girl's family or a Mithun" (2008: 3).

Another key customary law is the inheritance of moveable and immoveable family property. Daughters/women in the family are at the mercy or under the goodwill of the father or brothers or, if none of them, the clan male members. Inheriting family property solely depends on whether her father (or brother) is willing to share/give. According to the Paite customary law, the first son inherits his father's property (family property). If the father has no sons, but daughters, the family property can only go to the daughter, if the father made the will or announcement in the presence of the family *"Indongta"* during his lifetime.

"Indongta" is a family council in every household that takes up the family matters. The members comprise family elders and members from the husband's clan. It comprises nine members, out of which only three are women, known as the *"tanupis"*. The *"tanupis"* are the sisters of the husband. If the husband does not have any sister, women from his clan members are appointed. Their role and responsibilities are solely for the purpose of "labour" such as cooking and serving food on family occasions.

In matters such as rape, it is unfortunate that many cases were "settled" after the *"Indongta"* of both the parties mutually came to an agreement, which is usually a fine - by cash or kind - as a punishment of the accused. The Paite customary law states that a rapist will be fined five mithun (this in monetary term will come to about rupees 10,000) and one pot of wine. The understanding of justice is, therefore, confined to a settlement of the issue, or an agreement between the two parties' representatives.

Like many women across the globe, Zomi women are no exception in their body being used as a site of hatred and violence, specifically in a district like Churachandpur in which women were victims of communal or ethnic hatred and violence. On account of the aftermath of the infamous Tipaimukh rape case of 2002 and several other reported rape cases, the Churachandpur Joint Women Union (CJWU) was formed by various tribe-based women organisations. They resolved that punishment for rape accused should be a minimum of five years imprisonment, along with the traditional fine.

Moreover, it is a known fact that Zomi women were never the head of the traditional systems, such as chieftainship; neither were member of the traditional village council. Very few women have begun to be inducted in the modern system under the village authority. Given the very low number of women's participation, the quality of participation in decision-making is still a long way to go.

One of the biggest Churches in south Manipur, the Evangelical Baptist Convention (EBC), a congregation of about 51,201 memberships and 148 local Churches (2008 census), has no woman pastor (local priest). There are no woman in the key executive, functioning bodies. There is a segregated *"Dorca Pawl"*, women department that exclusively deals with women's affairs. Therefore, women's participation in the EBC is limited or restricted to the women department.

"Thohlawm", a collection of cash and kind and welfare, is one role and key function of the women department. Not surprisingly, the EBC Church administration headquarters in Lamka is famously named "Dorcas Hall". The infrastructure was reportedly constructed from resources generated and contributed by the Dorcas (women department).

Women and women department or organisations in any sphere of socio-cultural set-up, including the Church, were fondly called the "backbone" and not the head. Their contribution to the society is acknowledged, but unfortunately, their role is restricted to being a mere contributor and supporter.

Gender is a constructed concept of a dividing line of man and woman-based on the notion of "feminity" or "masculinity" and character associated with it, such as fair, long hair, and roles of doing household chores, respecting men, etc., for the female. Roughness, should not cry, etc., for the male. The biological difference between a man and woman was thus politically manipulated and socially "legalised". In ethnic/ indigenous societies, it was regarded/accepted as a custom and tradition.

Gender-based discrimination eventually creates inequality between man and woman, placing the woman in lower status to man, be it in the family, the society and political spheres. Cutting across communities, religion and class, it is reflected in varying forms, contexts and practices of a given society or group and values attached to these are at times specific to a particular cultural context. Socio-cultural or customary practices such as bride price or male inheritance in "tribal societies" is found in the form of dowry, *sati*, child marriage, etc., in so-called "mainland" India. In more developed nations or the West, the women are yet to take up the political leadership. Even the United States of America still has not had a woman president.

For instance, as Sindhu Phadke (2008) observed, every housewife is expected to perform the task of cooking and feeding. In earlier generation, if a wife shows alacrity in keeping *"zu"* (rice beer) for her husband when he wishes to relax with friends, she would be rated as a dutiful wife and hospitable hostess. In today's context, the devoted good wife would be preparing tea or food or attending to her husband and his friends' needs. Sindhu noted, laws are not codified and it is in the form of conventions in North-East India. Women's status is, thus, reflected in the manner in which laws or conventions are interpreted.

Some popular sayings amongst the Zomis go as *"Numei pilna in saangkil kanlou"* (a woman's wisdom does not go beyond the door), *"Numei in beh neilou"* (a woman does not have a clan), *"Numei vaak hat thusia zong"* (a woman who loiters around is looking for trouble). Such sayings reflect the perception of a woman in the society, how they are viewed and regarded.

A society such as the Zomis of North-East India follows or practises patriarchy where man is the head of family and descent/lineage, and eventually the head of the social and political structure.

V. Geetha in her book, *Patriarchy,* a series on theorising feminism, stated, "Patriarchy system rests on the defined notions of masculine and feminine, and is held in place by sexual and property arrangements that privilege man's choices, desires and interests over and above those of women in their lives and is sustained by social relationships and cultural practices which celebrate hetero-sexuality, female fertility and motherhood, on the one hand, and valorises female subordination to masculine authority and virility, on the other" (2007: 8).

Geetha further elaborates that patriarchy is not only the rule of men over women, but over younger and subordinates socially or economically including males (*e.g.,* caste system). She mentioned that matriarchy—the absolute rule of women over men and the society—was considered primitive and patriarchy a more advanced stage of existence. Thus, this primitive matriarchy, believed to be in existence before patriarchy, can be linked with the mythical belief of imaginary figures or deities and goddesses.

Matriarchy is assumed/perceived to be in practice among some of the "tribal" societies like the Khasis, Jaintias and the Garos of Meghalaya in NE India. Matrilineal system, where clan names are passed on from mother to children followed by these communities, was misunderstood as matriarchy. It may be noted that in Khasi society, male members are the overall decision-maker and authority in family and society at large. Therefore, given the "assumption" and its "primitive existence", it can be stated that matriarchy is a myth.

Conclusion

Gender-based perception, which attributes unequal status to men and women, is universal. The Zomi women are no better off than their sisters in the other parts of the world. There has been a tremendous change from the earlier generations and the contemporary in terms of women coming out from the confines of their kitchen and their homes. However, it may be underlined that this is basically limited to education and economic spheres. The highly patriarchal society such as the Zomis further enhanced by the strong traditional and religious institutions continues to hinder their progress to be in par with their male counterparts.

Another perceived notion is that women empowerment is a fight against men. Moreover, there has been a tendency that an "empowered" woman imitates man, which can term as a tendency to go the patriarchal way of life. It should be understood that gender equality or women empowerment does not mean "fight against men" or "fight against institutions", but a change in perception, attitudes and correcting some of the wrongs, in concepts and institutional practices. This will go a long way in the process of evolving a democratic system amongst the Zomis.

References

2013: *"Paite Pupa Ngeina Dan Leh a Kizatnate (2-Vei Puahphatna, 2013)"* [The Paite Customary Law, (2nd amendment, 2013)], available at *http://www.zogam.com/articles/educational/1439-paite-pupa-ngeina-dan-leh-a-kizatnate-2-vei-puahphatna-2013.html*, viewed on 14 January 2013,

Geetha, V (2007): *Theorising Feminism: Patriarchy* (Calcutta: STREE).

Hanghal, Ninglun (2010): "Regional Remorse in Mainland Metros", *The Statesman*, Kolkatta, 8th November.

Hanghal, Ninglun (2011): "Women Fight Violence in North-East Indian State", *One World South Asia*, 22nd November.

Hanghal, Ninglun (2012): "Street Fighting Years: How NE Women Cope with the Big City", *The Statesman*, Kolkatta, 11th August.

Kamkhenthang, H (2002): *The Traditional Customs and Rituals of North-East India* (Vivekananda Kendra Institute of Culture).

Official website of Evangelical Baptist Convention, *http://www.ebc-india.org*.

Official website Government of Manipur, *http://manipur.nic.in*.

Phadke, Sindhu (2008): *Women's Status in North Eastern India* (New Delhi: Decent Books).

6

Gender Inequality among the Kukis of Manipur

Lalgin Chongloi

Introduction

As gender issues have become more mainstreamed in scientific research and media reports, confusion associated with the terms, sex and gender, has decreased. In sociology, these terms are now fairly standardised to refer to different content areas. Sex refers to the biological characteristics distinguishing male and female. This definition emphasises male and female differences in chromosome, anatomy, hormones, reproductive systems and psychological components. Gender refers to those social, cultural and psychological traits linked to males and females through particular social contexts. Sex makes us male or female. Gender makes us masculine or feminine. Sex is an ascribed status because a person is born with it, but gender is an achieved status because it must be learned (Lindsey 2011: 4).

Gender also determines the range of choices/options open to men and women. These choices are linked to work and the production process, to mobility/seclusion, dress and behaviour and so on. The cultural, social and political practices of a society that are reflected in the sexual division of labour, role allocation and stereotyping, property and inheritance, distribution of authority and governance, and, most importantly, the unequal concentration of power and status among men and women in the society are the real expression of its gender construction (Kumar and Varghese 2005: 23).

Gender inequality is a form of inequality, which is distinct from other forms of economic and social inequalities. It dwells not only outside the household but also centrally within it. It stems not only from pre-existing differences in economic endowments between women and men but also from pre-existing gendered social norms and perceptions. Gender inequality hampers the overall well-being of a person because blocking women from participation in social, political and economic activities can adversely affect the whole society *(http://www.azadindia.org/social-issues/genderinequality.html).*

In this paper, an attempt is made to highlight the persistence of gender inequality in the contemporary Kuki society, with special emphasis to property and law of inheritance. The term "Kuki" is used to refer only the Thadou speaking community of the Kuki.

Status of Kuki Women

In traditional society, a woman had no rights in the family and society. She belonged in body and mind, from her birth till her death, to her father and brother before her marriage and to her husband after marriage. Women possessed nothing even though they did most of the work within and outside the house. The following sayings clearly testify the inferior status of woman in the past, *viz.,* (i) The wisdom of a woman does not extend beyond the banks of a river; (ii) A woman (wife) and old fencing can be replaced any time; (iii) Let women and dogs bark as they like; (iv) Women and crabs have no religion, etc. (Dena 2008: 36).

The women perform the role of a wife, mother, child bearer, food producer and household manager. They have wide responsibilities, ranging from household maintenance to various agricultural activities. They are held responsible for the proper maintenance of the family. Should the family prosper and the children do well, they earn the respect of the people. However, if the family falls on hard times due to mismanagement of domestic affairs, the women bear the brunt of ill repute. Clearly, the onus of domestic management falls on the shoulder of the women (Longkumer 2009: 119).

One of the important factors where status of Kuki women can be understood is a distinct role played by men and women. As a patriarchal society, father is head of the family. He exercises authority among members of the family concerning family affairs. It is his responsibility in sustaining and maintaining well-being of the family—in the fields of economy, education, health and others—assisted by his wife. The family members are dependent on him, but this dependency is reduced once the children are in a position to shoulder responsibilities of their parents. As head of the family, all important decisions such as children's education, marriage, property, issues relating to customary law, family economy and others are made by the father in consultation with his wife. Besides these, the father represents his family on many other important issues.

The wife assists her husband in running the family. She is responsible for all household chores, be it cooking, washing, cleaning and others. Though she has a right in the affairs of the family, she is normally ignored by her husband. There might be instances where she could influence her husband in taking important decisions. However, in general, her opinion is rarely taken into consideration. Therefore, there is disparity in the status and roles between the husband and wife in Kuki family.

The Kuki society holds the view that married women acquired full membership to her husband's family only when she conceived a male child. This is evident in the customary practice of claiming *"loungman"* (corpse price). According to Haokip (2011), *"longman"* is an indication that women are given importance and downgraded their status at the same time. *"Loungman"* is claimed in such a way that if the mother of an ego dies, the brother of the former claims the price of his sister's corpse from her son or husband who is his *"tucha"* relatives. However, in case of a woman who does not have a son, the *"sunggao"* (maternal uncle's family) relative cannot claim *"loungman"* from his *"tucha"*. This *"loungman"*, signifies that a woman does a great service to the family to which she is given in marriage by giving birth to a son(s), thereby, the genealogy of that family moves on and the generations of the male line spread further (Gangte 2010: 50-51).

It can be inferred that customary practice of claiming *"loungman"* clearly distinguishes between men and women. Women were undermined and considered being lower than men as her brothers or father could not claim her *"loungman"* if she did not bear a male child in her conjugal home despite the fact that she was a wife or mother or a daughter-in-law of that particular family, who wholeheartedly played an important role for the welfare of family in her lifetime. This further testifies the patriarchal nature of the society where importance is being accorded to a male child. In the absence of a male child, she is being alienated of her basic right under the ambit of their custom. The preference of a male child as against a female clearly illustrates the lower status of women in Kuki society.

Institution of marriage among the Kuki is another aspect which exemplifies lower status of women in the society. Traditionally, women who married under negotiated forms of marriage are highly respected and appreciated. They became a source of inspiration and a role model for the younger girls. Yet, rites and rituals as well as the formalities associated with departure of a bride suppressed her, which in turn directly affected her status. However, these rites and rituals are no longer relevant in contemporary Christian society as they are totally abandoned by them.

Gangte (2010) opines that "the manner of sending off the girl is exactly the same as done to a woman when she dies, thereby equating the girl as dead to the family, which in real sense conveys the significance that hereafter the girl truly belongs to the groom's family for all practical purposes. It also indicates that now the girl has left her natal home, she should not think in terms of coming back through divorce or after quarrelling. She should take her conjugal home as her real home. In other words, she is discouraged to a degree to think that she still belongs to her parents. She should whole-heartedly devote herself to please her husband, parents-in-law and other relatives of her husband and build up her own home for prosperity without the slightest inkling of divided loyalty".

The societal attitude towards women is agonising. Her parents even expect her to be submissive in her in-laws' house. Parents mould their daughter in such a way that she considers it her duty to serve devotedly and sincerely her in-laws in spite of the problem she might encounter in their relationship. It is her responsibility to strengthen her marital bonding with her in-laws. This good endeavour by her may be disregarded or responded positively by her in-laws. If her positive gesture is responded negatively by her in-laws, the whole liability is still with her. She would be still blamed of creating hostility or misunderstanding and would be called as *"mou phalou"* (bad daughter-in-law), despite a great effort attempted by her.

It is depressing that she has to explore and mend her ways and, if fortunate enough, she would be accorded warmly and treated well by her in-laws. If unfortunate, she would not be welcome as a daughter-in-law where the consequences can be disastrous. However, it is good to encourage women to be devoted to her conjugal home and consider it as her very own for the welfare of the family. She is expected to be deeply rooted in her conjugal home and never expected to return back home, whatever the case may be. Nevertheless, it is her parents who always stood by her in times of trouble and hardships.

Gender inequality in Kuki society is also apparent in their customary law governing rules of divorce which sanctioned custodian of children, though it authorises penalty to defaulters. In patriarchal Kuki society, customary law always favours man. If a married woman committed adultery and resulted in divorcé, she forfeits all her *"thilkhen"*, that is, marriage gift she brought with her at the time of marriage. She also forfeits custodians of her children. Her parents should also reimburse the principal bride price to her husband's family.

On the other hand, if the husband committed adultery and resulted into divorce, he should be penalise with a fine of one mithun and the principal bride price is not obligatory to be reimbursed. In this case, the wife has the right to claim all her *"thilkhen"*. But regrettably, custodians of the children remain with her husband. Thus, the Kukis are subjective with a perception that children always belong to father, thereby, undermining the position of women.

In religious spheres too, status of Kuki women is lower to men. "Religion has been a source of power for women or a source of subordination. The Church plays an important role in relations to women's welfare and status in general as various denominational Church councils have specific women's departments which look after the welfare of women in Church. Though, the Church has done immense work to uplift the status of women, yet certain restriction are also imposed like ordaining women as reverend and pastors. The idea of women being the head of religious institution is still frowned upon and unacceptable among the Kukis. Thus, even if women do become Church leaders, men do not favour the idea of women occupying the highest position in the Church" (Haokip 2011: 135-137). There have been instances of a woman being ordained as a minister in the Kuki society. However, when the ordained minister got married, objections were raised. Such objections are not raised with reference to male ordained minister (Haokip 2011: 107).

Nevertheless, the role played by mother or woman in their *"insung maicham"* (family prayer) and other religious activities is significant. Generally, it is the woman who supervises and coordinates all prayer activities in her family, thereby, inculcating moral values and good ethics to her children in particular and family in general. It is a rare thing to see woman as head of the Church and it may sound peculiar among Kuki society as it is very unusual to them. Their thoughts are embedded in such a way that they absorbed ethics of patriarchal values where according to them decision-making and head of institution belong only to men. Despite significant contribution made by women in religious spheres, it is yet to be acknowledged by the society at large.

The customary law of the Kuki sanctions rights only to men with regards to decision-making in administration of the village, customs and culture. This is evident in their traditional institution of *"haosa"* (chieftainship) and *"Kuki Inpi"* (apex body of the Kuki). The institution of *"haosa"* is the backbone of Kuki society, which is not transferable but hereditary through male line, *i.e.,* the eldest. *"Kho haosa"* (village chief) is head of the village in whom lies highest decision-making authority within the village. As head of the village, his life and actions are embedded with a spirit of *"khankho"* (humanitarianism). Hence, he wholeheartedly helps *"meithai chaga"* (widow and orphan) and other poor families of his village.

However, it is pertinent to note that in contemporary Kuki society, the spirit of *"khankho"* may not be possessed by *"kho haosa"*. His actions and ideology-might be a boon as well as a bane for *"chaga"* (orphan). All problems within the village which cannot be compromised and settled by the party concerned are brought to the court of *"haosa"*. The *"kho haosa"*, along with his *"semang pachong"* (cabinet member), study the cases thoroughly and make a final decision accordingly without biases to any of the group, though fair decision is fast disappearing in the present society of the Kukis as favouritism tends to become a common feature. In the institution of *"haosa"*, women can never become the chief of a village nor can she become a member of village authority.

"Kuki Inpi" is also a male-centric institution. Women's participation in *"Kuki Inpi"* is very rare. Though *"Kuki Inpi"* looks for all round development and welfare of the Kukis, women were never elected as the member. Ovung (2009) has pointed out, "Women were ignored in most of the important functions. They were not given rights to represent any clan, village decision matter. Though the tribal women dominate in socio-economic activities, their participation in the political processes and governance is practically nil. No woman has ever become the head or chief of the village. Thus, in the traditional system women are debarred from the decision-making body of the society".

Acquiring self-identity is another important factor of determining if gender equality exists in the Kuki society. It is observed that Kuki women struggle to acquire identity as they are normally recognised through other members of her family, *i.e.,* male members. For example, through her sheer perseverance and dedication, woman might bring laurels for her family in particular and society in general. Yet, they struggle to obtain their own identity as they would be acknowledged or recognised by the society depending on their marital status.

In contrast, Kuki men were liberated from struggling to acquire identity as they were recognised by their own. They did not require to be recognised through other members of the family. In fact, the social status of men determines female position in their family. Ironically, it is observed among women that whenever they try to learn the identity of other women, the question they raise among themselves is "Whose wife is she?" instead of, who is she? Or "Whose daughter is she?" The desire to know their husband's/father's name, instead of their mother's, reflects the patriarchal mind-set of the community.

In spite of their low status, the Kuki women figure prominently in the routine of domestic work and cultivation. The women are always very hard working. They have too little time available for leisure. They had to rise at dawn while the men slept on. Starting up a fire, they began to husk the rice and then make way down to the spring to fetch water with empty bamboo tubes. They collected the harvest rice from the fields and firewoods from the jungle. Apart from cooking, they looked after domesticated animals and birds like pigs and fowls. They prepared clothes for all members of the family. Their presence in the family is indispensable. Though women played a vital role in the family, men folk looked down upon and had low opinion of them (Lalrimawia 1995: 17-18).

Property and Law of Inheritance

Property is one of the basic requirements of any society. We often think of property as referring to an object(s). Strictly speaking, property refers not just to an object but also to the rights that the owner of the objects has in relation to others who are not owners of the objects. Property rights are backed by the state and enforced through its legal system (Rao 2010: 386). Though property ownership may be of many kinds as public, communal, private, individual, etc., it's most important aspect is the reference which in any of its forms it has to human personality. And this is so true that property may rightly be considered as a function of personality without which it cannot be properly understood but with this it has to share in the same problems and puzzles with which personality itself is involved. Property, the natural sequence of work, has always been present in mankind, though in widely different degrees, as far as we can ascertain. The idea that property is a universal phenomenon that it has existed in every known society is held without exception by every modern sociologist and anthropologist (Gisbert 1975: 149-150).

Ownership of property may vary from one society to the other. As in the case of native of North-Western Melanesia, husband and wife have each his or her own possessions. The wife owns her grass petticoats, of which there are usually some twelve to twenty in her wardrobe, for use on various occasions. The water vessels, the implements for dress-making, a number of articles of personal adornments are also her own property. The man owns his tools, the axe and adze, the nets, the spears, the dancing ornaments, and the drum, and also those objects of high value, called by the native *Vaygu'a,* which consists of necklaces, belts, armshells, and large polished axe-blades. Immovable goods, such as garden-land, trees, houses, as well as sailing-vessels are owned almost exclusively by men, as is also the livestock, which consists mainly of pigs (Malinowski 1929: 20-21).

Every society makes some provision for the transfer of property and social position on death and the transfer is usually to a kinsman. A son may inherit the property of his father. For example, if his father was a king, he may succeed him on the throne. A good deal of any legal system, including our own, is concerned with laying down rules about who may succeed whom – to titles of nobility, for example, and who may inherit what from whom–usually property of some kind, but also obligations and duties (Fox 1966: 16).

In the case of the Kukis, property can be classified into movable and immovable, self-acquired and inherited property. The movable properties consist of all the household items, domesticated animals and others. The immovable properties consist of a house, land, trees, etc. The selft acquired properties can be of both movable and immovable, so as the inherited properties.

In the primitive Kuki patriarchal society, the right of ownership belonged to the male. Men continued to be the sole owner of immovable properties and inheritor of ancestor property. Inheritance in the Kuki custom descended through the male line. Only the sons could inherit the property. Women were very much discriminated as they had no right to claim/ inherit property. When a widow remarries a man of another family, she forfeits the properties of her dead husband. The women lived an insecure life in the traditional Kuki society. In the absence of a male heir, the nearest male relative inherited the property and property may be distributed to other sons as well (Haolai 2006: 85-86).

The right of inheritance of the father's property, however, is based on seniority within the descent system. The descent system provides the structural basis for maintaining order. So long as bonds of kinship unite most members of the community, the system remains effective. The eldest son of the family assumes the responsibility of looking after his aged parents. Along with inheritance of the family property, the eldest son cannot neglect the moral obligation and duties that go along with it. The younger sons may establish themselves in different villages and houses, but custom rules that the eldest son sees to the welfare of the parents' house and assumes responsibility for unmarried sisters (*Ibid*: 75). The law of inheritance among the Kukis is so rigid that property could be passed on only to son. Thus, the eldest son get the lion share and inherits almost all the property of his father and he has authority to decide the amount of property to be given to his younger brothers in consultation with his father. Daughters were completely isolated or excluded in the fields of inheritance as a result. In absence of a son in the family, property would normally goes to nearest male kin or *"phung upa"* (clan elders).

It is observed that many of the parents having no male son wish to pass on their property to their daughters instead of giving to the nearest male kin. Their desire could seldom materialise as they were bounded by the customary law which is endorsed by the society. They were compelled to obey the law. Property may be passed on to the nearest male relatives called *"agam ngah"*, at their inner heart they felt hapless and insecure as all the fruits of their hard work would perish in the hands of someone, who possibly will or will not be so closed in their blood relations. They are also aware that the person who would be inheriting their property may or may not be reliable towards their daughters in future.

Similarly, after the father expired, their daughters may not be brave enough to claim the property as custom does not favour them. But if the person who would inherit property of the family in absence of male child, possessed in him *"khankho"*, he can passionately perform his duty towards the daughters—support and stand by them in times of happiness or sorrow.

The Kuki women before marriage play a significant role in her family. She is often regarded as a pillar of the family's economy. She wholeheartedly toils for the welfare of her family. Through her untiring effort, she might make a tremendous achievement in acquiring property. It is interesting to state that she exercises control over the property she acquired only as long as she is unmarried. But once she gets married, she forfeits all the properties she acquired before her marriage.

If she wanted to take or claim the property she acquired to be her *"thilken"*, this she can do only through the consultation of *"upa"* (eldest male of the family). This clearly illustrates how they were subjugated and concealed by customary law.

"Thilken" play a significant role among Kuki women as customary law of inheritance favours only a male child where the law forbids women to inherit ancestral property. Therefore, at the time of marriage, women could be given any forms of property by her parents, relatives and friends as a *"thilken"*. The rich parents may give their daughters a number of valuable properties at the time of her marriage. Ironically, the woman can forfeit all her *"thilken"* if she is found guilty of committing adultery. In cases of divorce where the husband is at fault, though women were entitled to claim back all her *"thilken"*, they often go empty handed as they felt powerless to do so. Instead, the husband retained all the property.

As in most patriarchal societies, a son inherits the father's title and property. The Kuki customary laws empower the son to be the head of the family. The daughter cannot assume headship or inherit her father's property. Deeply entrenched in this traditional patriarchal set-up, the Kuki society is yet to achieve a more equal gendered social structure. Surprisingly, even the literate and educated Kukis are not totally free of these partisan views. Sexist attitudes mould and shape their thinking. A biased father or even mother would, given the choice, prefer a son than a girl child. It is not an unfamiliar sight to see the birth of a son being celebrated with the ceremonial slaughtering of a pig amidst great rejoicing. The mother is praised to no end for giving birth to a male son, as if she had any say in this procreation. Discrimination of a girl child begins at birth as her entry into this world is often greeted with a chorus of disapproval (Haolai 2013: 32-33). The law of inheritance, which favours the male child, is still rigid in the present Kuki society.

Customary laws and traditional values have always favoured patriarchy. It may be impossible to do away with patriarchy and patrilineal system. Though men and women are different by nature, there is enough space to treat them as persons having the same rights and duties. It requires genuine efforts from both men and women to create a society where each person is given opportunities to live a fuller life (Kekhrieseno 2009: 110).

Conclusion

The principle of patriarchal value is entrenched in Kuki society where differences of rights and obligations between men and women were deeply rooted in their custom and culture. Women were discriminated and subordinated in every sphere of life. "As a child, a girl is subject to the authority of not only the elders, but all the male adults of the household. After marriage, she is subject to her husband and as a divorcee, she cannot claim her children; they belong to the family of husband. Woman remains in perpetual wardship, a widow is also cared for by her eldest son" (Haokip 2011).

However, it is observed that societal values and people's perception towards men and women are gradually changing in the present Kuki society. The once static Kuki society has now witnessed a steady transformation under the influence of formal education, Christianity etc. As a result, the status of women has also improved immensely. The spread of formal education has further accelerated the transformation of the status of Kuki women. Parents' attitude towards their daughters has also changed in which due importance is given to their education which lead to the increasing number of educated women. Today, we could see many educated Kuki women working in different fields of professions. In many of the families, women are the bread earners. It is observed that women's opinion is valued today by the society.

Despite all these changes, patriarchal values are not completely wiped out as women are still considered subordinate to men. The Kuki customary law still favours men. Therefore, gender inequality is significantly visible where women are subjugated and their rights to property and inheritance are denied.

References

2013: *http://www.azadindia.org/social-issues/genderinequality.html*, viewed on 1st April 2013.

Dena, Lal (2008): *In Search of Identity: Hmars of North-East India* (New Delhi: Akansha Publishing House).

Dube, Leela (1997): *Women and Kinship: Comparative Perspective on Gender in South and South-East Asia* (New Delhi: Vistar Publications).

Fox, Robin (1966): *Kinship and Marriage* (London: Penguin Books).

Gangte, TS (2010): *The Kukis of Manipur: A Historical Analysis (Reprint)* (Delhi: Gyan Publishing House).

Gisbert, P (1975): *Preliterate Man* (Jaipur: Rawat Publications).

Haokip, Arfina (2011): "Position of Women in Kuki Society: A Critical Analysis", in Ngamkhohao Haokip and Michaeal Lunminthang (ed.), *Kuki Society: Past, Present and Future* (New Delhi: Maxford Books).

Haokip, Hoipi (2011): "Women in Kuki Society: Study on Working Women in Imphal Valley (East and West) Manipur", in Ngamkhohao Haokip and Michael Lunminthang (ed.), *Kuki Society: Past, Present and Future,* (New Delhi: Maxford Books).

Haolai, Thangkim (2006): *Kuki Culture in North Cachar Hills: Before and after the Advent of Christianity* (Guwahati: Joint Director, AIRT & SC).

Haolai, Thangkim (2013): "Status and Empowerment of Women in Kuki Culture", *Voice of the Hill*, 15th March – 15th April, 32-33.

Kekhrieseno, Christina (2009): "Inheritance and Gender Implications with Special Reference to the Southern Angami Group", in Kedelizo Kikhi and Narola Dangti Kikhi (ed.), *Changing Gender Equation with Special Reference to Nagaland* (New Delhi: Akansha Publishing House).

Kumar, Hajira and Jaimon Varghese (2005): *Women's Empowerment, Issues, Challenges and Strategies: A Source Book* (New Delhi: Regency Publication).

Lalrimawia (1995): *Mizoram: History and Cultural Identity* (Guwahati: Spectrum Publications).

Lindsey, Linda L (2011): *Gender Roles: A Sociological Perspective (Indian edition)* (Delhi: PHI Learning Private Limited).

Longkumer, Jungmayangla (2009): *Change and Continuity in Tribal Villages: A Sociological Study* (New Delhi: Akansha Publishing House).

Malinowski, Bronislaw (1929): *The Sexual Life of Savages in North-Western Malenesia* (London: Routledge and Kegan Paul Ltd.).

Ovung, Athungo (2009): "Status of Women with Special Reference to Naga Society", in Kedilizo Kikhi and Narola Dangti Kikhi (ed.), *Gender Equation with Special Reference to Nagaland* (New Delhi: Akansha Publishing House).

SECTION–III
DEMOCRATISATION VIS-À-VIS IDENTITY POLITICS/CIVIL SOCIETY/STATE

7

Identity Politics and Process of Democratisation

(Emerging Trends in North-East India)

Akhil Ranjan Dutta

This paper is an attempt to reflect on the critical inter-linkage between identity politics and democratisation, with special focus on its manifestation in North-East (NE) India. I will use the Bodo Territorial Area Districts (BTAD) violence of 2012 to illustrate my points of argument.

The BTAD in Assam that started in July 2012 raises serious questions about the democratic viability and accommodative capacity of an ethnically defined autonomous council in a multi-ethnic setting. Series of violence in 1990s in the Bodo Autonomous Council (BAC), which was created by Assam state legislature in 1993, and its reoccurrence both in 2008, and 2012 in the present day BTAD established under the Sixth Schedule of the Constitution, invites serious retrospection on desirability and risks of ethnically defined autonomous council which does not ensure adequate representation of the other communities in the Council.

Perceived to be a forward move towards democratisation, the ethnic movement in NE India has entered a very critical phase where the constitutionally empowered ethnic groups through autonomous councils, etc., have been targetting the other marginalised communities within the councils in an attempt to ensure the all round dominance for itself. In the process, the "co-strugglers", i.e., the marginalised communities who have been struggling for the same sort of rights and self-determinations are now turning into co-enemies. In case of BTAD, the aggressive elements from within the Bodos have been targetting the non-Bodos, particularly the Bengali origin Muslim settlers inside BTAD.

The formation of the Bodo Territorial Council (BTC) has facilitated flow of funds under a number of schemes. This has also created challenges for a tribal community like the Bodos, which had more of a communitarian economy rather than a money-based economy. The growth of a ruling class in a tribal community and contestation and conflicts within them to capture state power, the phenomena which is relatively new for a tribal community like the Bodos has also put challenges and has broken down the communitarian and egalitarian structures of the community. The state with its proclaimed goal of "national integration" has thrown open these communities to such vulnerabilities and manipulations where a community like Bodos, which is a culturally rich ethnic community in Assam, is becoming very obsessive and intolerant in nature.

Ethnicity and Nationality in North-East India: BTAD Violence in Perspective

The UNDP in its 2004 Annual Human Development Report, entitled *Cultural Liberty in Today's Diverse World,* has pointed out that the identity politics has emerged as the new mode of political articulation in the contemporary world. It argues, "In vastly different contexts and in different ways, from indigenous people in Latin America to religious minorities in South Asia to ethnic minorities in the Balkans and Africa to immigrants in Western Europe-people are mobilising anew around old grievances along ethnic, religious, racial and cultural lines, demanding that their identities be acknowledged, appreciated and accommodated by wider society" (UNDP 2004: 1). The UNDP has also pointed out that these movements are not isolated. "They are part of a historic process of social change, of struggles for cultural freedom, of new frontiers in the advance of human freedoms and democracy" (*Ibid*).

However, at the same time, the UNDP has also warned that if struggles over cultural identity are left unmanaged or managed poorly, they "can quickly become one of the greatest sources of instability within states and between them and in so doing trigger conflict that takes development backwards. Identity politics that polarises people and groups is creating faultlines between 'us' and 'them'. Growing distrust and hatred threaten peace, development and human freedoms" (*Ibid*: 2).

The UNDP has also pointed out the danger of the mobilisation of group identities which adopt coercive methods against others. The UNDP quotes, *The Economist* (2000) to elaborate the point which states, "Leaders of movements for cultural domination build group identities and mobilise their followers to adopt coercive methods against others. Leaders use their organisational skills to gain supporters, modify ideologies to suit their needs, arrange finances at home and abroad and give weapons and training to militant cadres. Such leaders pursue two core aims: creating an ideology of intolerance and altering the balance of political power." The Report also says, "The easiest way to breed intolerance is to use self-serving interpretations of history to describe and vilify other groups. By doing so, leaders emphasise the quest for justice and focus on the losses their group allegedly suffered. The focus is not on solving real grievances but on using ostensible grievances as rallying cries" (*Ibid*: 77).

It can reasonably be argued that BTAD violence in Assam was an outcome of poorly managed politics over ethnic identity as well as mobilisation of group identities both on genuine as well as ostensible grievances.

Ethnicity and nationality are two important dynamics of Indian politics. It is to be noted that both ethnicity and nationality are closely linked to each other. Ethnicity is a cultural entity. An ethnic group is marked by homogeneity in language, culture, traditions, patterns of livelihood, food habits, etc. When such a group asserts for political recognition and demands separate political entity in the form of autonomy, statehood, etc., then the ethnic group converts itself into a nationality. In this sense, the ethnic politics is indeed the politics of nationality. Politics of nationality in India and also in many other countries has raised the demand of right to self-determination. The politics of nationality and right to self-determination has been described as "symphony of freedom" by the radical political forces (AIPRF 1996). For example, Manoranjan Mohanty, a theorist of peoples' rights and right to self-determination argues:

> "The Indian Union that had come to be managed as a centralised polity has been successfully challenged by autonomy movements. The Report of the Sarkaria Commission on centre-state relations, whose recommendations for federal practice are yet to be implemented, was an acknowledgement of the emerging demand for democratic restructuring of the Union. The people's movements in Kashmir and Punjab, in the North-Eastern states, in Jharkhand, Uttarakhand and Chhattisgarh acquired such serious dimensions that the Central government had to make occasional concessions to the people's demands. The formation of an autonomous council in Gorkha areas of Darjeeling in West Bengal, the Bodo autonomous council in Assam, the Jharkhand area autonomous council in Bihar are some examples. But the main approach of the rulers of the Indian state continues to be one of the coercion and repression through army and paramilitary forces, by resorting to 'draconian black laws' which power the security forces to take arbitrary measures such as indiscriminate arrests, torture and killings in false 'encounters'. Yet, one thing has become clear. The self-determination movements have succeeded in putting the nationality question on the core agenda of politics which the rulers cannot ignore. The Indian Union

has to be restructured and democratic aspirations of the nationalities have to be fulfilled" (Mohanty 1996: i).

It needs to be reasserted that the politics of ethnicity and nationality is the outcome of the nation-building process in India. The over-centralised federal polity has failed to recognise and accommodate the culturally specific rights and aspirations of the multitude of ethnic communities in India, particularly in North-East India. The national movement in India could not reach out and integrate many of the ethnic communities in the country into the project of the Indian nationhood. The Constitution of India envisaged various provisions like Article 370 for Jammu and Kashmir and Sixth Schedule to accommodate the aspiration of the ethnic hill tribes in NE India. However, such limited autonomy had been decried by many ethnic tribal communities in the region on the ground that it miserably failed to recognise and appreciate the historically enjoyed independence by them. As a reaction to such failure, the ethnic assertion emerged as the real driving force of politics in India's NE. Historicising the problem in NE India's context, political scientist, Sanjib Baruah argues :

"At least if one goes by the number of political organisations whose names clearly indicate ethnic agendas, the nature of ethnic mobilisation in NE India today is quite extraordinary. Even those of us living in NE India may not have heard of all the ethnic groups in whose names various liberation struggles are being fought. But, as students of history and politics, we should not be surprised by this phenomenon. After all, if ethnic mobilisation is about the politics of recognition, (Taylor, 1994) to say that others may not have heard of the Karbis or Tiwas of Assam or Hmars or Zomis of Manipur is to entirely miss the point of ethno-national political mobilisation. The fact that not many people have heard of them or if they have, they have misrecognised them may, at least partly, explain why their leaders feel the need to make their existence known and to proclaim the way they wish to be recognised" (Baruah 2004: 7).

It is in this particular historical context that the entire political landscape of North-East India today is dominated by ethnic assertions and conflicts. In the region, ethnicity has emerged as prime political mover. In Assam itself, the assertions by ethnic communities like the Bodos, Karbis, Dimasas, Deoris, Rabhas, Mishings, etc., are important trend-setters in the political dynamics. These ethnic communities in the region have mobilised themselves on ethno-cultural lines demanding autonomy, statehood as well as secession from India. Most of these ethnic groups do have their insurgent outfits too. The government has tried to address these assertions through various means. The Sixth Schedule of the Constitution with a provision of a territorial autonomous council was envisaged to accommodate the dissents of the ethnic hill tribes in NE India.

However, in 2003, the Bodos, a plain tribe of Assam, had also been offered a territorial council, named BTC, under Sixth Schedule of the Constitution covering four districts of the state. In 1993, the Bodos were granted Bodo Autonomous Council outside the Sixth Schedule of the Constitution. With the creation of BTC, the NE India has the following autonomous councils under Sixth Schedule of the Constitution.

In Assam: The North Cachar Hills District Autonomous Council (NCHAC), known as Dima Hasao, as nomenclature was changed on 30th March 2010; The Karbi Anglong District Autonomous Council (KAAK); and The Bodoland Territorial Area Districts (BTAD).

In Meghalaya: Khasi Hills District Autonomous Council (KHAC); Jaintia Hills District Autonomous Council (JHAC); and The Garo Hills District Autonomous Council (GHAC).

In Mizoram: The Chakma District Autonomous Council (CDAC); The Mara District Autonomous Council (MDAC); and The Lai District Autonomous Council (LDAC).

In Tripura: Tripura Tribal Areas District Autonomous Council (TTADC).

Apart from the Bodos, other plain ethnic tribes in Assam like Mishings, Rabhas, Tiwas and Deoris have also been demanding "right to self-determination". To accommodate their dissent and demands, the Government of Assam created three non-territorial autonomous councils in 1995, and three more had been created in 2005 for the Mishings, Rabhas, Tiwas, Deoris, Sonowal Kacharis and Thengal Kacharis. These non-territorial councils have now demanded the status of Sixth Schedule after the Bodos were granted the same in 2003.

The right to self-determination, demanded by the ethnic communities, has entered a critical phase in North-East India today. The conflict in BTAD in 2012 has been an eye opener in this regard. These kinds of conflicts, however, had occurred earlier too in other Councils. The Bodos had to wage a long struggle to achieve the territorial council under the Sixth Schedule of the Constitution. The movement in its heyday demanded a separate state for itself and the demand is still alive. Although the Bodo is a homogeneous ethnic community, there are factions within them contesting for power.

The most important challenge in an ethnically defined autonomous council is how the council accommodates and protects the interests of the other minority ethnic communities within the council. In BTAD, the Bodos constitute 34 per cent of the total population. Remaining communities constitute 66 per cent. Important among those other communities are Konch Rajbongshis, Santhals and the Bengali origin Muslims. As the autonomous council had been given in the name of the Bodos, there were protests from the non-Bodo communities. Such protests had arisen mostly due to the demographic composition in BTAD. In case of some of the villages that fall within BTAD, the non-Bodos constitute the majority. These communities have alleged that their rights have not been duly taken into consideration while forming the BTC. There is also substantial number of East Bengal (now Bangladesh) origin migrant population inside the BTAD. Some of these people came to Assam during the colonial period, during partition and also after Independence. It is alleged that there are substantial number of Muslim migrants who came after 1971. Substantial number of Bengali origin Hindus had also migrated after 1971. They are all illegal migrants as per the Assam Accord, 1985. Most of the pre-1971 migrants, although, are Bengali origin, most of the Muslim migrants have accepted Assamese as the mother tongue as revealed by the successive censuses.

It is to be noted that the continuing influx of migrants from East Pakistan and later on from Bangladesh provoked the six-year long Assam movement which culminated in signing of the Assam Accord on 15th August 1985. Ideologically, the movement was a non-violent one. However, aggressive and chauvinist elements were active in the movement. The Hindutva forces tried to influence the course of it. As a result, gross intolerance and aggressiveness became part of the movement here and there. It was due to such aggressiveness that the infamous 1983 Nelie massacre in the present-day Morigaon district had taken place, which took lives of 3,000 Muslim peasants. These Muslims were suspected to be Bangladeshis (Engineer 2012). It was one of the worst human tragedies in the history of Assam/India. Though the Assam Accord accepted 1971 as the cut off year to detect and deport the illegal migrants from Assam, the Accord has not sincerely been implemented and there are allegations that the influx still continues. It is against this background that there is growing apprehensions in regard to the presence and increase of illegal migrants in Assam.

In BTAD too, there is substantial number of Bengali origin migrant population. There is no authentic data in regard to the exact number of illegal migrants, either in Assam or in BTAD. The Bodo people, including the BTC authority, have been alleging that there has been encroachment of land by the illegal migrants in BTAD. It was under such an environment of both real and perceived insecurity that the conflict between the Bodos and the Muslim migrants occurred in 2012, which took around 100 lives and rendered around four lakh (four hundred thousand) people homeless from both the communities. The 2012 conflict is not the first of its kind. In 1990s, the Bodo militant outfits had undertaken a mission of "ethnic cleansing" against the immigrant Muslims and the Santhals in the present-day BTAD, which also took hundreds of lives and rendered thousands of people homeless. In 2008 too, there was violence between the Muslims and the Bodos, which took more than 50 lives and rendered thousands of people homeless.

During 1994 and 1995, such operations were first tried against the immigrant Muslims, which is one of the most vulnerable communities in the area. However, from 1996 onward, the operations were launched mostly against Santhal peasants, another marginalised group of post-colonial Assam. Capturing the unabated violence against the marginalised communities within the present-day BTAD during 1990s, Subhash Barman writes:

> "The Bodo-Muslim conflicts of October 1993 cost many lives and 3,568 families comprising about 18,000 persons were rendered homeless in Kokrajhar district. A series of major conflicts again took place throughout the Kokrajhar district in May 1996, when 42,214 families comprising 202,684 persons were rendered homeless. They were forced to take shelter in 61 relief camps. This time the operation was carried out against one of the most vulnerable communities in Assam, i.e., Santhal peasants. Violent activities again flared up in May 1998, and thousands of people were forced to leave their home. It must be remembered that the violence perpetrated by the Bodo extremists did not target only non-Bodos. Several noted Bodo political leaders and intellectuals, who spoke out against the indiscriminate killing by Bodo militants, also lost their lives in the hands of the militants. A sense of fear of being killed or injured became an existential reality in the area, particularly among the marginalised groups" (Barman 2009: 223-24).

The following chronology of conflicts may give a sense of danger attached to ethnic homelands in North-East India.

(i) October 1993: Bodos and Muslims clash in Kokrajhar and Bongaigaon where 18,000 people were displaced; (ii) May 1996: Violence between Bodos and *adivasis* in Bongaigaon displacing 262,682 persons; (iii) September 1998: Ethnic conflict between Bodos and *adivasis* in Bongaigaon displacing 314,342 persons; (iv) September-November 2005: 43,819 persons were displaced in clashes in Karbi Anglong between Karbi and Dimasa tribals; (v) August 2008: Conflict between Bodos and Muslims in Darrang and Udalguri where 200,000 persons were displaced; (vi) March-May 2009: Dimasas, Nagas clash in North Cachar hills, displacing 11,737 persons; (vii) January 2011: Rabha-Garo conflict displacing over 50,000 persons; (viii) July 2012: Bodo-Muslim clashes displacing 392,000 persons. Before this round, 180,000 internally displaced people living in camps: 33,600 in Kokrajhar, 13,722 in Bongaingaon, 120,545 in Darrang, 11,737 in North Cachar Hills (Mitra *et. al.* 2012).

BTAD Violence 2012

The 2012 violence in BTAD that appeared to be sporadic in nature in the beginning has now proved to be systemic and endemic. It is no longer the emotional and spontaneous outburst of a community against another community perceived to be illegal invaders. The violence has been captured politically by the communal and reactionary forces and thereby has made the reconciliation a distant dream. Neither the Bajrang Dal nor the Muslim communal forces that had steered the Mumbai violence in the name of protection of the Muslims in BTAD have anything to do with the life and livelihoods of the hardworking common people from whatever community in BTAD.

BTAD is a multi-ethnic, multi-cultural homeland. The Bodo is a culturally rich ethnic community in Assam and it has pride in its own identity. Like any ethnic community having commitment to its self-esteem, the Bodos too had reacted both peacefully and violently against the insult and discrimination meted out to them, both by the dominant Assamese nationality and the Indian state in the past.

However, in the process, the emerging middle class from within the Bodos had also been co-opted by the Indian state with the motive of weakening the strength of unity and resistance inherent into their culture. It is to be noted that the Bodos were never as divided as it has been after the BTC Accord was signed in 2003. The formation of Bodo Peoples' Progressive Front (BBPF) just after the signing of the BTC Accord was one of the most glorious moments for the Bodos. BPPF was an opportunity to create a culture of reconciliation both within the Bodos and also between the Bodos and the other communities living in BTAD.

That glorious historical opportunity had collapsed with the intervention of the political forces; particularly the Congress led state government. Had the alliance between the All Bodo Students Union (ABSU) and Bodo Liberation Tigers (BLT) for a peaceful and prosperous BTAD through the entity of BBPF survived and sustained, probably the situation in BTAD for the last one decade would have been radically different. The division within the Bodos had given the communal and reactionary forces, mostly from outside, to penetrate into the politics in BTAD. Left into one's own cultural dynamics, a community cannot be so violent for violence is not inherent to any community as such. It is true in case of the Bodos too.

Who then are to be blamed for the violence in BTAD today? The Muslims in BTAD? Definitely not. The common Muslims who have been living in the present-day BTAD for decades together are mostly hard working peasants. There have also been migrations of Bengali origin Muslims to the BTAD, particularly to Kokrajhar from the Char areas of the neighbouring districts who are displaced every year by flood and erosion. There may be post-1971 migrants among these Bengali origin Muslims. However, all these migrant labourers cannot be labelled as Bangladeshis. The economy in BTAD has evolved a dynamic of interdependence between the Bodos and the Muslim peasants. Most of the migrant Muslim settlers work as cultivators in the land owned by the Bodos and also as domestic help with them. This has happened in the historical process of the emergence of a middle class and with the increase of organised political activism within the Bodo community. When large number of the youths is involved in political activism or gets themselves involved in petty business, it is natural that it invites migrant labourers to work in the paddy fields.

Many of the Bodo families have started informal leasing out of land to these migrant labourers. Once the number of such leasing out increases, more and more migrant labourers enter in these Bodo villages. Under such changing situation, there has evolved a unique pattern of villages in some areas inside BTAD where adjacent to the Bodo villages, the migrant Muslim labourers have settled down and gradually evolved into villages. The Bodos in such villages even indulge in advance sale of fruits of their homestead gardens to these Muslim settlers. The Muslim peasants also work as petty marketers in such villages.

How such a marginal community conspires against the Bodos and steer violence? And in whose benefit will they do it? They definitely understand the consequences. They can do it only at the risk of their own peril. If it is so, why the Muslims should tolerate the communal forces in Mumbai who through their irrational act have brought both misery and insecurity to them in BTAD? Asghar Ali Engineer has unequivocally blamed these communal forces from within the Muslims for such detrimental acts to the peace loving and hard working Muslims in BTAD. He also asked how a religious Muslim could do it in the month of *Roza*? If they wanted to do something for the peace in BTAD, Engineer argues, they should have prayed for the peace of all victims across religions. They should have come forward to help both the Muslims and the Bodos in the relief camps. They did not do that. Rather, they communalised it to the extent that a local issue of violence has become a communal tension for the country as a whole. Are these forces operating in BTAD?

Probably, "yes". But, are the common Muslim peasants responsible for this? Definitely not. Their bread and butter are safe in a peaceful atmosphere in BTAD.

However, there are certain other points which invite serious scrutiny. The Hindutva forces are very strong in Gujarat, Karnataka and Maharashtra. In Karnataka and Gujarat, the BJP is the ruling party. In Maharashtra, Shiv Sena has strong presence. Therefore, it is very hard to believe that some notorious Muslim elements can be so powerful to push thousands of youths and students of North-East India out from these states. What did these Hindu forces and the governments in those states do while such threat perceptions were spread through nook and corner of the respective states? Did these Hindutva forces also connive with the communal and reactionary forces for political mileage? Communalism has no religion, although communal forces work in the name of religion. Communalism is the greatest threat to democracy and composite and social fabrics of the society. It is particularly relevant for a multi-cultural context of BTAD.

Today, the BTC administration is arguing that had the BTC been given more powers to deal with the law and order situation, it could have handled violence promptly and efficiently. It implies that the law and order has not been enforced promptly and efficiently by the responsible authority. Law and order is a responsibility of the state government and, at least partly, the violence is an outcome of the failure of the state government to handle the situation promptly and efficiently. Why has it happened so? It is now believed that the law and order was unconstitutionally left into the hands of the BTC. It has been argued that the police administration was not very sure who the appropriate authority was in BTAD to be reported for any law and order related incident in BTC. Had it been a non-Congress government, the Centre would have exercised its authority to discredit the state government for such a constitutional failure. The alliance of the Congress-led state government with BPP-led by Hagrama

Mahilary is, therefore, responsible for the situation. Had there been no such alliance, the state government would have been in a position to ensure the universal surrender of arms by the erstwhile BLT cadres. Unauthorised possession of arms by these cadres and to counter the same, the procurement of arms by other groups in BTAD has made the situation worse.

Hagrama Mahilary has been asserting that the violence in BTAD has been caused by forces from outside. He is pointing fingers at the illegal migrants from across the border. The state government is not in agreement with such arguments. Central government's position is not very clear on the issue. Such confusions and non-convergence among different layers of the government has created more insecurity in BTAD. Inordinate delay to update NRC has provided fertile ground for Hindu communal forces. A government which fails for years together to develop a consensus on the format of NRC updating does not deserve to be called a responsible government.

Land is supposed to be the most important issue behind the conflict in BTAD today. It is true that there had been transfer of land from the tribals to the non-tribal communities. However, it appears to be an exaggeration that it is only the Muslim migrants who have invaded the land in BTAD. But, the threat perception prevails. Therefore, the issue immediately needs to be addressed and tackled. However, as has already been pointed out, there has also been informal leasing out of lands by the Bodos to the Muslim peasants for cultivation. By such arrangement, a pattern of interdependent economy and livelihood evolved in BTAD. Has such arrangement itself fuelled violence in BTAD? If it is so, the pattern itself has to be addressed with political foresightedness.

The National Commission for Minorities (NCM) visited the conflict hit BTAD in July 2012, and warned that "there is a possibility that Muslims in the Bodo districts of Assam will turn 'militant', influenced by *Jihadi* outfits from across India, in case their security is not ensured by the state government" (Ali 2012). The Commission pointed out three important dimensions of the conflict, namely, (i) The present conflict in BTAD "was not between some exodus of Bangladeshi immigrants and the Bodos", but between the Bodos and the resident Muslims of the BTAD; (ii) The conflict was unequal in nature. Compared to the heavily armed BLT cadres, the Muslims were poorly armed; (iii) It cautioned regarding potential *Jihadi* influence in future on the Muslim population in Bodoland, which will make the conflict very intensive and dangerous. There can be grave danger in future in case militant *Jihadi* outfits from the rest of the country start supplying lethal weapons in this area" (*Ibid*).

What is to be noted here is that the BTC Chief, Hangrama Mahilary, attributed this conflict to the illegal migrants from Bangladesh, i.e., terming the tragedy as externally steered. For example, in an exclusive interview given to Anand Soondas, *Times of India* and published online dated 25th August 2012, Mahilary said the solution to BTAD conflict lies in throwing out illegal immigrants. "There is a permanent solution: throw out illegal immigrants. They should be pushed out and action should be taken against them". He is also of the view that growing Bangladeshi population threatens "Bodo culture, their way of life and peace" in BTAD. But it is not confined only to BTAD. "It is a threat to the country's entire north-eastern region. It has to be taken seriously by all parties concerned" (Soondas 2012). Mahilary is also of the view that it is only the Muslim radical groups which are creating problems in BTAD and in the country. "There are no other radical groups playing mischief here except HUJI, Muslim United Liberation Tigers of Assam, and United Muslim National Army. They are bent upon creating problems not just here but throughout the country." Assam's Chief Minister, Tarun Gogoi, however dismissed Mahilary's claim that there are two lakh illegal immigrants in BTC.

Mahilary is not alone in this line of argument. Sudheendra Kulkarni, member of the national executive of BJP also called it 'Indians vs. foreigners' conflict. On 27th July 2012, he posted a paper online with the title "It is not a Hindu vs. Muslim conflict in Assam, but Indians vs. foreigners" and argued:

> "At press time, nearly 50 people had been killed and above 200,000 people have been rendered homeless in prolonged communal-ethnic violence in and around Kokrajhar district. Violent clashes have broken out between native Bodos and illegal Muslim migrants from Bangladesh. The root cause of this violence is the joint failure of the federal and Assam state governments to stop wave after wave of Bangladeshis from swarming into different parts of Assam and drastically charging the state's demographic profile, especially of the districts close to the border. In Bodo populated areas, this 'flood' has caused large scale usurpation of tribal lands and made Bodos feel fearful that they are being marginalised in their own land. There is a well-known word for it—ethnic cleansing. What is happening in Assam, and it has been happening for decades now, is ethnic and religious cleansing caused by this massive human flood" (Kulkarni 2012).

This right-wing propaganda has very forcefully been negated by secular Muslim intellectuals like Asghar Ali Engineer. In his fortnightly piece, dated 1-15 August 2012, published by Centre for Studies in Society and Secularism titled *Assam and Bodo-Muslim Clashes: Reasons and Analysis,* Engineer wrote:

> "The right-wing BJP had added much fuel in propagating that Bangladeshi Muslims are migrating in large numbers giving highly exaggerated figures without any basis. Today, there is widespread network of RSS since eighties and it has been systematically working there to create cleavage between Hindus and Muslims though historically there has been communal harmony between Hindus and Muslims and in creating this harmony Shankar Deo, on the one hand, and Azan Fakir, on the other, have played a very important role" (2012).

The indigenous Assamese speaking Muslims, on the other hand, are not ready to accept it as Bodo-Muslim conflict as they are not part of the conflict at all. Assam's indigenous Muslim communities, the Gorias and the Morias, have accused All India United Democratic Front (AIUDF) chief, Badaruddin Ajmal, of communalising the violence in BTC areas, leading to mass exodus of North-East people from different states in India.

The indigenous Muslim communities, under the banner of Sadou Asom Goria Moria Deshi Jatiya Parishad (SAGMDJP), equally blamed Hindu, Muslim and Christian fundamentalist forces for trying to wedge differences among different indigenous communities during the BTAD conflict. The SAGMDJP also demanded the arrest of Ajmal, alleging that he took the initiative of giving the Bodo-Muslim conflict communal colour (Mitra 2012). It may be noted that a section of the indigenous Muslim community has been forming a joint platform with that of some tribal groups which is now demanding the cancellation of the Assam Accord and to fix the cut off year as 1951 as against 1971 as agreed upon by the Assam Accord for detection and deportation of foreigners from Assam. Mention may be made here that a conscious section of the indigenous Muslim community rejects such assertions and they do not accord their approval to such platforms which will create more fragmentation within the greater Assamese society.

The Konch Rajbongshis, who have also been affected by the violence, consider themselves to be "the forgotten victims of Bodo-Muslim crossfire" (Roy 2012). In a mixed camp, an elderly Rajbongshi inmate lamented, "It is not just Bodos and Muslim, we are also suffering. We said nothing. Why did our houses burnt? Tell me why do the newspapers not talk about us?" (*Ibid*). "The Rajbongshis have become the collateral damage of what has been characterised as a Bodo-Muslim conflict. These refugees feel that they get scant attention from anyone...Ironically for the Rajbongshis, their earlier conflict had been with the Bodos during the Bodoland uprising in the 1980s and 1990s. Now, the latest clash makes them feel that their position is even more tenuous" (*Ibid*).

It is amidst these developments that several organisations, including O-Bodo (non-Bodo) Surakshya Samiti, demanded the review of the BTC Accord terming it as a Himalayan blunder. The organisation is of the view that the Bodo Accord has created "a favourable condition for permanent ethnic clashes in Lower Assam districts" and has also provided "political encouragement to the chauvinist forces to launch ethnic cleansing drives" (*The Assam Tribune* 2012).

Yasmin Saikia argues that in Assam two narratives run parallel. The first is the "inclusive philosophy of *manabata* or humanity/humanism" and the other is an "exclusionary rhetoric of *bideshi* or outsiders/strangers". Saikia has pointed out that:

> "the narrative of *manabata or* humanity expresses a spirit of accommodation and is represented in Assam's blended culture encapsulated by the slogan of *'xanmiholi'* allowing diverse religious, ethnic, linguistic and cultural groups to find their location within the Assamese society. The other narrative of *bideshi*, however, speaks of "Assamese fear, anxiety, and inhospitability towards others." She wonders 'how does the stranger become transformed into an enemy, an objectified Other, against whom violence is socially legitimised." She has also pointed out that "the concept of legal (core) and illegal (disposable) groups that has taken root in Assam as a result of the careless use of term *bideshi* by politicians and public alike needs to be evaluated for understanding the transformation of 'outsiders' as enemy. The recent violence between the Bodos and Muslims should be placed within this conceptual map" (Saikia 2012).

In BTAD viclence today, Saikia asserts, the first philosophy is almost absent. It is only second narrative i.e., the narrative of "fear, anxiety, and in-hospitability towards others" is operating there.

All these narratives reveal the very complex nature of the BTAD violence in Assam. However, the key to violence is the manipulation of the state to delegitimise the genuine demands and to co-opt the elites of the ethnic communities into the fold of the state power structure and the obsessive and chauvinist tendencies within the dominant ethnic communities. The obsessive and chauvinist tendencies are, however, the replica of these tendencies exhibited by larger or dominant nationality groups like the Assamese nationality during 1960 language movement and also during six-year long Assam movement.

Where Do We Go from Here?

The violence in BTAD has evoked resurgence of protests against the illegal migrants throughout the state of Assam. Today in the nook and corner of the state, thousands of people are coming out on the street demanding immediate implementation of Assam Accord and detection and deportation of Bangladeshis. The protests are emotionally charged and it may deteriorate into communal offensive if adequate precaution is not taken by the government and also by the secular and democratic civil society in the state. The indigenous Assamese speaking Muslim community in the state is part and parcel of the Assamese culture and literature and their assimilation into the greater Assamese society is a foregone conclusion. These Muslims have nothing to do with the political mobilisation of the East Bengal origin Muslims in some districts of Assam (districts of Dhubri, Goalpara, Barpeta, Nagaon, Morigaon, etc.) by Badaruddin Ajmal-led AIUDF.

It is to be noted that the AIUDF had won 18 seats in the 126-member Assam legislature in 2011 election. The Assamese speaking Muslims have no vote bank in the state and, therefore, they do not have a separate political voice. The voice of the greater Assamese society is also their voice. However, a section from within this community has also developed a sense of insecurity amidst the emotionally charged political mobilisation and erosion displaces every community and makes the lives of the common extremely miserable. In September 2012 alone, the wave of devastating flood displaced around 20 lakhs people in Assam. Both the union government and the State government of Assam have exhibited their extreme insensitivity towards the miseries of the people. The Chief Minister of Assam was on an official tour to Japan when the devastating flood took place. Now, whereas the violence in BTAD that displaced mostly the Muslim migrants immediately occupied national headlines and forced all top political leadership to visit Assam, the devastating flood received no serious attention of the government at all. The issue was immediately communalised.

Non-convergence in Approach and Opinion among Different Layers of the Government on the Issue of Illegal Migrants

When the violence started in the BTAD, the three layers of the government—BTC, State government and Union government—had started speaking differently on the issue of presence of illegal migrants in the BTAD. Whereas the BTC chief, Hagrama Mahilary, counted the presence of illegal migrants in the BTAD in lakhs, State government attempted to deny the presence of illegal migrants altogether. The Union government expressed its serious concern over continuing influx of Bangladeshis through the porous borders. Such a non-convergence in approach in regard to the issue of illegal migrants created political hue and cry in the state. Therefore, convergence must be achieved across all layers of the government on the issue. Denial of presence of illegal migrants by any layer will intensify apprehensions. Assam Accord must be implemented with due sincerity. It is the responsibility of the government. Union government has the highest responsibility in this regard. If Assam is to be saved from a 2002 Gujarat like situation, the implementation of the Accord is a must. The NRC updating and border fencing should be the two most important priorities.

Marginalisation of Decent and Critical Voices within Bodo Community—Role of the Government

Due to wrong policies of the government, the moderate and critical voices are gradually disappearing from the public domain in the Bodo society. The Bodo society is also divided into many factions. Any critical voice is treated as anti-Bodo. This is one of the serious challenges for the Bodo community having long-term implications. A society prospers through critical voices. There are still some moderate voices, which are to be searched and strengthened. Only such an endeavour can create communal harmony in the BTAD.

Whose Responsibility is Law and Order? The Issue of Illegal Possession of Arms

Law and order is a responsibility of the State government. However, it was left into the hands of the BTC. The BTAD is a multi-ethnic homeland. Leaving law and order into the hands of the BTC has created fear psychosis among the non-Bodos in the BTAD. The BTC cadres, who have not yet surrendered arms, have created more problems. It is believed that to confront the situation the other communities, particularly a section of the Bengali-origin Muslims, have also acquired arms. The government must ensure universal surrender of illegally acquired and possessed arms.

Illiteracy, Poverty and Birth Rate: The Political Reaction

Among the communities in Assam, the East Bengal origin Muslims are the poorest, illiterate and flood and erosion effected. Marriage at lower age, high fertility rate, religiosity and illiteracy all are inter-connected problems. There is a growing perception that these people give birth to more children with a hidden agenda to make Assam a part of Bangladesh. Although illogical, the issue is sold like a hot cake. The government has to take the issue seriously. Along with addressing the issue of flood and erosion, the people in the Char areas have to be provided with both modern education and health-care facilities. Family planning among the illiterate Muslims is opposed on the ground of religious prohibition. Ilias Ali, a professor in Gauhati Medical College and Hospital, has taken personal initiative for a family control campaign among these Muslims in Char areas. Initially, Ali faced a lot of resistance. Gradually, these illiterate Muslims are welcoming Ali's initiatives, which are yielding positive results. Such instances are to be capitalised by the government.

The Secular Foundation of Assamese Society

Despite communal offensive from time to time such as 1960 language movement, Neille massacre, etc., the secular foundation of the society in Assam is still strong. It is for this reason that the communal forces have failed to establish solid and sustaining foundations in the state. Assam is known as the land of Shankar and Azan, the two saints Shankardeva, a *Vaishnavite* religious reformer, and Azan Fakir, an Islamic prophet. *Zikir,* the song that praises Allah, is an integral part of Assamese music and culture. In Assam, the party like BJP has failed to communalise the society. Rather, the BJP has been forced to be secular at many instances. It is the strength of the society in Assam. The organisations like Bajrang Dal and Vishwa Hindu Parishad have been condemned by the nationalist forces, including All Assam Students Union (AASU), who is still steering the movement against the Bangladeshis in Assam. The government should take help of all these forces.

Progressive and Secular Community in Assam and its Historic Role in 1960s

In 1960, when Assam was boiling on the language issue, the then Chief Minister, Bimala Prasad Chaliha, invited Hemnga Biswas, a communist cultural activist, leader of Indian Peoples' Theatre Movement (IPTA), to take up a cultural mission in the affected areas. It had tremendous impact. Bhupen Hazarika and a number of progressive cultural activists took part in it. There are a number of organisations in Assam, which are still working on the same lines. They may not be supporter of the Congress or the government, however, they will give a helping hand once given a chance. In Guwahati, the secular forces have mobilised opinion against the communal offensive once the BTAD violence started. This year, Assam has been celebrating the Birth Centenary of Hemanga Biswas. Different progressive organisations have been holding meetings and cultural programmes on the occasion. These occasions have been used to condemn any communal offensive and campaign in the pretext of protests on the issue of illegal migrants in the state.

Dissent in Other Issues should Sincerely be Addressed

There is a general perception that North-East India's resources-tea, oil, coal, mines and now water are exploited by the Centre and corporate forces. On issues like large river dams, there are growing apprehensions in Assam. For the first time in Assam's history, the peasants have come on the streets in the capital city of Guwahati, both on the issue of large dams and land rights. Commissioning of large dams in NE India has been perceived as selling out of the water resources to the corporate sector. The government should address these apprehensions. Demand like cumulative impact study before commissioning the large river dams should immediately be undertaken.

Accommodating the Rights of the Non-Bodos in all Ethnically Defined Councils Including in BTAD

The organisation like United Reservation Movement Council of Assam (URMCA) demanded that the BTC Accord be immediately withdrawn. Such a demand is not justified. It will only intensify violence in the BTAD. The BTC, with whatever limitations, is an outcome of decades of movements of the Bodo community. The Accord has also intensified conflict within the Bodos, particularly between two factions, Bodo Liberation Tigers (BLT) and All Bodo Students Union (ABSU). At many instances, these are state steered manipulations. Such manipulations have paid heavy prices.

The government must consider adequate representation of the minority communities in the ethnic councils.

Finally, it is only through a secular approach-based on the principle of people's security that the violence of the kind that Assam has been passing through can be prevented. Here lies the role of the civil society, the secular and progressive forces in the state. These forces have to forcefully engage themselves in public domains continuously exposing the communal and chauvinist tendencies.

References

Ali, Mohammad (2012): "Bodoland Muslims Might Turn 'Militant,' Warns Minorities Plan", *The Hindu,* 16th August.

Barman, Subhash (2009): "Conflict-induced Internal Displaces and their Ssecurity: A Case Study of Lower Assam", in Akhil Ranjan Dutta (ed.), *Human Security in North-East India: Issues and Policies* (Guwahati: Anwesha), 219-233.

Baruah, Sanjib (2004): "Historicising Ethnic Politics in North-East India" in Girin Phukan (ed.), *Inter-ethnic Conflicts in North-East India,* (New Delhi: South Asian Publishers), 7-24.

Chandra, Bipan *et. al.,* (2000): *India after Independence, 1947-2000* (New Delhi: Penguin Books).

Dutta, Akhil Ranjan (2012): "Struggle for Life and Livelihood: The Doyang-Tengani Forest Dwellers' Movement in Assam" in Nani Gopal Mahanta and Dilip Gogoi (ed.), *Shifting Terrain: Conflict Dynamics in North-East India,* (Guwahati: DVS Publishers), 33-62.

Dutta, Akhil Ranjan (2012): "Indian State and Colonial Apparatuses: Can Peace be Achieved in North-East India by Violating Peoples' Rights?", *Indian Journal of Political Science,* April-June, LXXIII(2): 283-98.

Dutta, Akhil Ranjan ed. (2009): *Human Security in North-East India: Issues and Policies* (Guwahati: Anwesha).

Engineer, Asghar Ali (2012): "Assam and Bodo-Muslim Clashes: Reasons and Analysis", *Centre for the Study of Society and Secularism,* 1-15 August.

Kulkarni, Sudheendra (2012): "It is Not Hindu vs. Muslim Conflict in Assam, but Indias vs. Foreigners", posted in rediff.com news, viewed on 27th July 2012.

Mitra Dola, Debarshi Dasgupta, Uttam Sengupta (2012): "A Bridge Too Far", *Outlook India*, 13th August.

Mitra, Naresh (2012): "Assamese Muslims Slam Ajmal for 'Communalising' Violence in BTC Areas", *The Times of India*, Guwahati, 18th August.

Mohanty, Manoranjan (1996): ''Resounding Symphony of Freedom'', *Symphony of Freedom: Papers on Nationality Question* (Hyderabad: AIPRF), I-XIXI.

Roy, Sandip (2012): "Rajbongshis, the Forgotten Victims of Bodo-Muslim Crossfire", *Firstpost. Politics*, 6th August.

Saikia, Yasmin (2012): "Blame 'Em, Bludgeon 'Em: Assam's Violence has Grown around Suspicion of 'Outsiders'", *Outlook India*, online version, viewed on 13th August.

UNDP (2004): *Cultural Liberty in Today's Diverse World* (New Delhi: Oxford University Press).

8

Identity Issues and the Emerging Reality in North-East India

Gorky Chakraborty

Introduction

During the major part of the 20th century, the spread of "modern" with its elements of industrialisation, democracy and nationalism was featured to bring about modernity and a sense of national identity, which would subsume all other identities, including ethnic. And thus "for more than 40 years following the World War II, few new states were created through ethnic secession... only two new ethnic states emerged: Singapore and Bangladesh". However, during the close of the same century, "more than 10 ethnically defined states have emerged". Ethnic identities as well as conflicts now play an important role in determining various facets of international relations which are manifested in many conflicting zones around the world.

Why has there been a shift in patterns of mobilisation, struggle and their various manifestations? Is it a phenomenon of the pre-modern expressing it in post-modern forms? Or were these roots of ethnic mobilisation entrenched within the utopia of modernity? Analysing these questions and related issues may throw some light to understand the contemporary reality in North-East (NE) India.

From Archaic Space to Territory

The pre-capitalist space of contemporary North-East has been a bio-region of numerous clans that was a relatively closed system, which was primordial in nature occupying varying geo-spatial areas with clan and kinship boundaries. The economy was subsistence-based and the political structures were largely self-contained with multitudinous social and political formations ranging from the republican, authoritarian to the convivial systems determined by their respective stages of economic formations. During the subsequent period of colonial administration, this clan-kinship spatiality of the ethnic communities was intruded with colonial spatiality that resulted in deconstruction of the erstwhile community space.

The colonial spatialisation of the archaic space got initiated from the strict stand-point of *terra incognita,* which eventually was transformed into *terra cognita.* Introducing the private property regime to capture the commons and resources of this archaic space became the hallmark of colonial spatiality. Colonialism annihilated the hitherto existing primordial spaces through capital movement and military aggression and simultaneously recreated colonial space for market, raw materials and surplus accumulation. This initiated the emergence of colonial administrative boundaries, which were often incompatible with the ethnic boundaries of the clan-kinship spatiality.

By re-defining the role of chiefs and institutionalising the same according to the requirement of the colonial imperative, the chiefs became the custodian of such spatialisation. The annihilation of archaic space, with the creation of colonial space, was manifested through various events starting from the Treaty of Yandaboo (1826) to the Government of India Act, 1935, which termed the backward tracts in Assam into "Excluded" and "Partially Excluded" recreated spaces mainly to serve colonial machinations of "an administrative border", a frontier of active protection" and an outer "strategic" frontier.

Colonial spatiality thus made the ethnic space spherical, eroded the ingenuity of the primordial social, economic and political institutions, fractured the ethnic categories and also hindered their primordial mobility and exchange. Such spatialisation gave the colonials a relative advantage through managerial, political, legal and resource controls over the recalcitrant tribes in the frontiers and, on the other, territorial localisation of the ethnic spaces on vertical heights. i.e., hills, which did not necessarily coincide with ethno-cultural boundaries of the hill people in all cases. This had adverse ramifications in the post-colonial era.

The social pathology emanating from colonial spatialisation was perpetuated in the post-colonial era where the post-colonial spatial reconstruction turned out to be more critical vis-à-vis the colonial era. The state building project of India largely reproduced the spatial boundary lines drawn by the British and, notwithstanding anything to the contrary, such borders and boundaries were considered important markers of the sovereign territory of the nation state. The symbol of nation, after Independence, was surcharged with power that upheld a homogenised and mono-cultural national identity that gave rise to subordination of the ethnic groups, thereby letting loose the pent up frustration among them. This led to ethnic movements and the failure of the Indian state to economically integrate the North-East problematised the issue further.

A major cartographic reconfiguration of the North-East happened in the aftermath of the partition of the country. The borders and boundaries were redefined under the newly emerging nation-state of India. The North-East in the process became largely cut-off from the rest of India and, ethnically, its continental connection with Myanmar and later Bangladesh, Bhutan and Tibet became restricted. The grievances of the ethnic groups against alleged internal colonisation of the Indian state found spatial expression with the separation of several areas from Assam. What started with Nagaland ended with declaration of statehood to Arunachal Pradesh, of course, in between punctuated by the North-East Reorganisation Act, 1972. This spatial configuration continues till date in the region under different constitutional provisions and administrative arrangements.

From Politicisation of Ethnicity to Ethnicisation of Politics

Spatial reconfiguration, starting from the colonial to the liberal era, has been accompanied by another feature, i.e., identity formation. The anti-colonial struggle in the Indian sub-continent has certainly had a multiplier effect in this direction. However, contradictions were apparent since the days of Indian Statutory Commission (1927-30) that various population groups in the region were apprehensive about their status in the emerging nation, i.e., Independent India. Not only the Assam Government constituted a seven-member committee to co-operate with the Commission, but there were also twenty-seven memoranda submitted by various population groups belonging to the hills and the plains in the region. This indicates that the apprehension palpable among the population groups later on led to autonomy aspiration during the liberal era.

While a sense of distinct identity and a consciousness, thereby, was not new to the hill people as their "economic-political-cultural arrangements were not disturbed either by the Ahom rulers in parts of present-day Assam or the British" vis-à-vis the plains, it was the spread of colonial modernisation mainly through the expansion of "modern" education and the subsequent growth of middle class that identity consciousness became a rallying point in the plain areas. Although one might argue that consciousness about some sort of distinct identity was already there in the Assam plains, yet the difference lies in successfully consolidating this consciousness by the emerging middle class and rallying people for giving a definite direction to these perceptions.

With the passage of time, it was realised that identity consciousness alone was not enough to allay their apprehension of losing their identity along with maintaining their sway over their emerging territorial space. They graduated to use consciousness in the form of identity assertion within the system, which later on developed into demands for self-determination. The solution to this problem, according to them, was not always within the framework of the nation state.

On the other, it is observed that "due to specific historical and administrative traditions, the self-determination aspiration in the hills has been from the beginning political in nature – the Nagas, the Mizos, the Khasi-Jaintia-Garos, the Karbi-Dimasas – all began their assertions with a more or less definite political idiom". Contrarily, to begin with the assertion by the ethnic groups from the plain had a non-political focus (e.g., safeguarding cultural identity, preservation of language, choice of a script, instruction through mother tongue, etc.), which of course later graduated for a separate political identity. Thus, although there was a temporal variation among the ethnic groups in the region towards asserting their political identity, they almost moved in the same direction of self-determination.

The response by the Indian state to these movements of identity assertion and self-determination got complicated due to the lack of clear-cut policy. It fluctuated between treating them as mere "law and order problems" to be dealt with by security agencies or through palliatives of politico-administrative set-ups. Leaving aside the security onslaught [which continues till date and the continuation of the Armed Forces (Special Power) Act 1958 in the region is a blatant reminder in this direction], granting of the Sixth Schedule to the Constitution of India has remained an important benchmark to administer many areas of the NE.

Even the issues related with the Schedules for administering the tribal areas have an interesting history. The bottom line of the Schedule, based on the Nehruvian policy of tribal welfare and influenced by the ideas of Verrier Elwin, was that the economic life of the tribal has to be upgraded while protecting their culture. The colonial origins of this policy and the twist and turns in the position of Indian National Congress can be seen as the debate progressed from 1935 to 1950. In 1935, while the supporters of these Schedules argued for segregation of these people as the most effective way of modernising them, the nationalist anthropologists and Congressmen contested these assertions, as a means for promoting cultural primitivism and, thereby, roadblocks in the nation-building process.

The advent of independence saw an unusual twist in the debate. The Congress now started arguing in favour of the creation of the Schedules citing that the new nation required the forging of an identity that respected cultural pluralism. Therefore, it was natural that the integration of tribal into the national mainstream would be slow, and that they should be treated with tolerance and empathy.

On the other, what the forces of modernisation did through spread of education and emergence of middle class was spread and consolidated during the liberal era and, no matter whatever the intentions were during this era, the politico-administrative arrangements could not retain the egalitarian notions of the tribal societies nor could they recreate an arrangement that could upheld the tribal communitarian ethos. It was a compromise formula saddled with certain politico-administrative arrangements and liberal financial-grant palliatives. This arrangement suited the emerging middle class and this new political elite fashioned themselves in tune with the provisions of the Sixth Schedule and the norms of parliamentary democracy.

But this fashioning of the emerging elites into the post-colonial order came with a price and that was its severing of interest of the tribal masses at the cost of material well-being of a few. Thereby, the process that got initiated during the colonial period became widespread, both in its "reach" and "content", during the post-colonial order and the resultant effect was the rising inequality in access to ownership of land, resources and other means of production.

This had a two-fold effect in the milieu of the North-East. While many among the political elites continued to run the subsidised administration on the basis of liberal grants from the Union Government by means of a special category status. Others who confronted the statist construction of the nation with their narration of nationhood manifested the "rebel consciousnesses". Now, the NE region due to its geo-political location has always been viewed through the prism of security and a sense of threat perception bothered the Indian state and any further threat within the boundaries was likely to have severe repercussions. The rebel consciousness has, thereby, to be neutralised at any cost. While those among the elites, who chose to be a part of the system, erected a patron-client relationship with the Union Government and they fluctuated between the palliatives of the Indian state and the limits of tribalism. Maintaining the identity-based on culture became an important benchmark in this direction. But the fluctuation, on the other hand, within this dilemma was easier said than done due to which there has often been dislocation within the power structure which pushed the ethnic groups towards the rebel agenda.

While the process of modernisation resulted in politicisation of ethnic groups that generated the latent identity consciousness among them, which graduated towards identity assertion that ultimately created avenues for self-determination, the ethnicisation of politics in the region germinated faultlines and thereby a common platform of struggling ethnic groups in the region could not emerge. The lack of ideological bulwark, absence of inclusive agenda and a constructive long-term vision generated a bizarre situation where one ethnic group was pitched against the other in its effort of constructing a politico-administrative set-up and earning financial grant palliatives from the Union Government. The demand for political autonomy of one ethnic group ceased to be the quest for the highest common denominator of humanity where the autonomy demand of one ethnic group seemed to be a threat for another. This is generating a spiral where the quest for an ethnic nation vis-à-vis the state nation remains entrapped in a narrow vision where the latter hegemonies the former's space in the name of building the nation.

Points to Ponder

As we discussed in the earlier sections about the spatial configuration and its impact on ethnic identity formation during various historical periods, in this concluding section we will contemporalise the same during the neo-liberal era. In the contemporary neo-liberal frame, there has been a change in the discourse on ethnicity and nation state. The earlier administrative categorisation of the ethnic groups within the state-centric mode of spatiality is "constructed" to give way to extra-territoriality. But this re-scaling, essentialised by the market-based approach, seeks to include only the markers of ethnicity as a constitutive of market economy without considering the social space in which these ethnic relations are situated. In other words, the ethnic space is being reconstituted by market principles with a view to widen the consumer constituency. Thus, the political economy of globalisation seeks to de-essentialise ethnic space and recreate the same as an economic space to suit the designs of profit and accumulation.

In the contemporary era, the Look East Policy (LEP) roused a consciousness about the emergence of an economic space in the region through the expectation of global trade, communication and financial flow to the neighbouring countries and beyond. The reference about the continuity of the North-East space as a gateway to South East Asia is limited to economic interpretation and which misses the issues related to social and cultural implications of the same space, on which the entire edifice of economy, culture and literature of the ethnic communities is embedded. So, socio-cultural facets related to this ethnic space of the North-East became facile in the neo-liberal order.

However, there is a caveat here. While the Indian state in the Look East Policy shows an overwhelming intent to follow the inherent tendency of capitalism to annihilate space by time (i.e., to overcome geographical boundaries in search of raw material, labour and market) by opening the region for trade and commerce, the same state maintains a selective amnesia about recommending anything related to socio-cultural implications of the concerned people. Is there an ominous sign in-built into this situation? Will it redefine the paradigm of identity-based movements in these areas since three major constellations of ethnic groups, the Chin, the Zo and the Naga (along with the host of others) have been sufferer of a long and treacherous process of division of their ethnic space in order to suit the design of enacting the political boundaries of the nation states? History will bear the testimony to such a conjecture.

References

Datta, PS (1993): *Autonomy Movements in Assam* (New Delhi: Om Publications).

Prasad, Archana (2004): *Environmentalism and the Left* (New Delhi: Leftword).

Ray, Asok Kumar (2010): *Whither North-East?* (New Delhi: Om Publications).

Riggs, Fred W (2011): "The Modernity of Ethnic Identity and Conflict", available at *http://www2.hawaii.edu/~fredr/riggs.htm,* viewed on 12th July 2011.

Smith, Anthony D (1993): "The Ethnic Sources of Nationalism", in Michael E Brown (ed.), *Ethnic and International Security* (Princeton: Princeton University Press).

9

Ethno-nationalism in North-East India

(Examining Civil Society Engagement with Ethno-political Aspirations)

Roluahpuia

Introduction

The resurgence of civil society in Europe has put civil society in the academic realm. What was peculiar about it was the role played by civil society in bringing down authoritarian regimes, particularly during the 1970s and 80s. The revival of civil society owes much to the social movements. Today, civil society has made foray in academic and non-academic fields and received prime importance among them. Old ideas were revived and made alive, which was followed by newer debates and contestations.

The North-East (NE) India provides a composite picture of different realities. The region is known for numerous ethnic demands ranging from secessionist to autonomy movements. Interestingly, civil society of the NE has been forerunner in such movements. This paper attempts to engage the role of civil society in ethnic political aspirations in the context of NE India. It begins with a conceptual and theoretical understanding of civil society. This is followed by an overview of civil society in NE India and the role they play in ethno-nationalist movements. The paper then highlights the challenges facing the civil society of the region and ends with a concluding remark.

Civil Society: Conceptual and Theoretical Understanding

Civil society continues to be a debatable term, both at the academic and non-academic realms. Different scholars have attempted to define and/or understand the nature and dynamics of civil society, both at the conceptual and theoretical levels. To have a glimpse of what civil society means and the problems associated with it, we will look at various understandings that have emerged over time.

Michael Walzer (2003) argued that "The words 'civil society' name the space of uncoerced human association and also the set of relational networks formed for the sake of family, faith, interest, and ideology that fills this space". This is rather a simple definition and understanding of civil society. For Chandhoke (1995), civil society is that space where society enters into relationship with the state.

A very different understanding comes from the Marxist thinkers such as Gramsci (1929), who puts civil society as a mechanism of the bourgeoisie in maintaining their dominance and promotes the interest of the ruling class. According to this understanding, "elements of civil society are co-opted by the state and used to secure acquiescence of the dominated classes and identification with the hegemonic world order" (Katz 2006: 335).

At another level, civil society is seen as a "collection of individuals and collective initiative for the common public good". The common public refers to the initiatives which are taken by individuals or the community for the betterment of the common public. This "public good" could include promotion of education, health-care or sanitation; it could include prevention of human rights or maintenance of peace and harmony; it could also include expression of dissent (Tandon 2003: 64). This is because civil society is often equated or used as a synonym for the good society (Beteille 2001).

Our intention of drawing different definitions is to unravel the different ways in which civil society has been conceptualised by different scholars. Walzer's definition is directly in contrast to that of Gramsci and Chandhoke. Yet, none of the understanding is absolute, nor is there a universally accepted definition of it. One is prone to become lost in the complexities of the debate around the definition and be influenced by the assumptions of one understanding or the other.

Moving further ahead, a sociologist like Beteille (2001) sees civil society as that space of "mediation between the citizen and the state in modern democracies". As he notes, "Civil society nourishes not under totalitarian regimes but under liberal, pluralist and secularist regimes, and it is a defining feature of the latter that they accommodate diverse conceptions of the good society". He further argued, "A totalitarian regime accommodates partisans only of a particular political cause; a liberal regime accommodates partisans of different political causes". In such a setting, civil society "is an open sphere which not only permits differences but also tolerates dissent, and to a certain extent even encourages it" (Dhanagare 2001). This line of argument reflects the co-relation between civil society and democracy. In other words, it shows the strong link that civil society has with democracy. Both civil society and democracy are seen as a twin phenomenon and interdependent and democracy is considered to be central to civil society thinking.

It is pertinent to mention that civil society at the global level has been resurrected particularly with the political upheaval that takes place from the late 1980s onwards (Chandhoke 1995; Khilani 2002). It is for this reason that civil society has become a household term among academicians, intellectuals and activists having different ideological orientations. The concept became handy for intellectuals and activists of varied ideological persuasions (Jayaram 2005: 15) and "is on everyone's lips—government officials, journalists, funding agencies, writers and academics" (Chandhoke 2007: 608). It is for this reason that Jayaram (2005) calls civil society as a "rebound or recovery concept". From here onwards, civil society has made a new entry, particularly in the literature of political science. In fact, it has now become a buzzword and it is used more loosely than ever before. New conceptions and new understandings of the concept are given, which led to new debates and new contestations. But the single largest implication remains on the fact that it has been used often baloney.

As a loosely used concept, its fuzziness lies in the inclusion of institutions which may have different agendas, objectives, even ideologies to the extent of opposing ideologies or non-democratic institutions. Such an understanding simplifies the term, while on the other hand, adds to the problem in defining and delineating boundaries to what constitutes civil society. Yet, for some like Carothers and Barndt (1999-2000), civil society constitutes a wide array of organisations. As put by them:

> "Properly understood, civil society is a broader concept encompassing all the organisations and associations that exist outside the state (including political parties) and the market. It includes a gamut of organisations that political scientists traditionally label interest groups—not just advocacy NGOs but also labour unions, professional associations (such as those of doctors and lawyers), chambers of commerce, ethnic associations, and others. It also incorporates the many associations that exist for purposes other than advocating specific social or political agendas, such as religious organisations, student groups, cultural organisations".

However, this understanding also faces the same problem in terms of its legitimacy and its relation to the state. Here, the legitimacy is related to the question of the much-talked about "uncivility". In fact, the blanket application of the term "civil society" to represent such different and opposing organisations further muddled the issue. It is more problematic when one looks at such organisation from the perspective of its relation with the state. As noted above, some organisations are directly linked to the state. The glaring examples are NGOs, labour unions, etc., which are registered under the state framed laws and whose functioning is regulated by the state. Also, labour unions themselves are the arm of the political parties and, thus, they themselves become a part of the state apparatus. To quote Jayaraman (2005) again in the context of India, he says, "After all, in India too, the NGOs have to be registered and they need to observe the laws enacted by the state, and are even subjected to state control and audit". Therefore, there is a real problem in the lumping of institutions, organisations under one banner, that is, civil society.

The above discussion highlights the different interpretations in relation to civil society. Despite the numerous variations underpinning the understanding of civil society, the two key ideas which run through the understanding of it are: civil society is seen as an important space (mediation, mobilisation, etc.) between the State and the people, and Central to making democracy alive. Democratic upsurge with the downfall of authoritarian regimes has resulted into the equation of civil society and democracy. It is due to this that civil society is often seen as a harbinger of change from authoritarian regime to a democratic one. In the same way, civil society is seen to play a key role in ensuring the functioning and deepening of democracy. Yet, the notion of what constitutes civil society continues to be a contested terrain and is still a debated issue among the academicians, politicians and those who are directly a part of civil society.

Civil Society in North-East India: An Overview

In India in general and the North-East in particular, civil society in the form of various associations, both at the formal and informal levels, is widely seen. Many civil societies in the NE are grounded on primordial ties and almost all of them have their own ethnic names or titles attached to their respective bodies. These primordial features may include kinship, clans, tribe and religion. These bodies are more local in nature and limited to the community level in their functioning. The fact is that the communities of the North-East are tied by social bonds through institutions. These institutions can extend from philanthropic-based to Church-based, student bodies to women groups, etc. At times, it can even be organisations directly working with organisations, which are in direct opposition to the state. Civil society is not a new phenomenon in NE India. The region is indeed blessed with institutions and organisations, which are run and administered by the community themselves. At the same time, the region also has seen the rise of voluntary organisations known as Non-Governmental Organisations (NGOs) in the common parlance. Such organisations are now mushrooming in almost all the states.

On the very same line, we have a wide gamut of formal and informal associations in the region. The region has a number of organisations which bind together people of the same ethnic groups, be it youth groups, women-based organisations, faith and charity trust-based, etc. These bodies have their functions at the local level and play a crucial role on issues pertaining to the community at large. They take up collective issues and undertake various activities that have impact on the community. "This gamut of groups signifies that there are alternative forms of associations in the region that probably fill in the available spaces of non-violence, compassion and collective action for constructive work" (Banerjee 2009: 160).

There are also ethnic-based organisations which are the most predominant in the region. They represent the interests of the concerned ethnic group. Ethnic-based bodies can include Hmar Youth Association (HYA), Young Paite Association (YPA) and others of the same line. The ethnic component is reflected in the members of such organisations. That is, members of such bodies are those who belong to that particular tribe and ethnic group. From here, it is understandable that civil society in the NE is established along tribal and ethnic lines.

At the broader level, there are groups, which are more representative such as All Assam Students Union (AASU), All Tribal Students Union Manipur (ATSUM), Zomi Council (ZC), Young Mizo Association (YMA), Khasi Students Union (KSU), Naga Students Union (NSU), etc. These bodies are representatives of numerous tribes and communities and represent the interests of the larger society. In every state, no matter whether the communities are small or large, it is common to see local-based institutions. And for larger communities/nationalities like the Mizo, Naga, etc., such local-based groups have a linked at the larger level. Taking the case of the YMA, every Mizo village in Mizoram has its own YMA branch and every Mizo household is affiliated to it. However, these local bodies are directly linked to the bodies which operate at the state level. They operate under Central Young Mizo Association (CYMA) and their operations are guided by the norms and guidelines laid down by the CYMA, which is the apex body. The same is with the case of some Naga-based organisations such as Naga Hoho, Naga Mothers' Association, etc (Das 2007). They have their own federal set-up, which makes the body representative. More interesting aspect of these bodies is that they cut across political boundaries by operating across different states and even countries.

One critical aspect of civil society in the region is that they act as strong pressure groups. This is particularly true for most of the communities which are dominant in the state. They include communities such as the Meiteis, Khasis, Assamese, Mizos. In such situations, the respective state governments are bound to listen to the issues raised by such bodies. The case of the valley-based organisations in Manipur or the Meiteis' civil society organisations can be one such example of this. United Committee Manipur (UCM), All Manipur United Clubs Organisation (AMUCO), which have their base in Imphal are acting as a strong lobby group in enacting legislations. Such bodies confront the state to pass laws that they think will hamper their community's interests. They are also spearheading the movement against the political demands made by the tribals of the state. In more clear terms, whenever the bells of Sixth Schedule start ringing, organisations such as United Committee Manipur immediately enter into the scene and warned the governments, both the Centre and the State, against taking any steps or decisions that will affect the sentiments of the majority as well as the territorial integrity of Manipur.

Over the years, the North-East also saw the mushrooming of NGOs in the region. Although they are found to engage in various social and development issues, the impact of their functioning is yet to be felt. These bodies face numerous challenges due to the armed conflict problem, which in many ways limit their functioning. Most of the issues taken up by these organisations are one of the most serious, yet, often neglected ones in the region. A very simple, yet major dissimilarity between some of the ethnic-based groups and NGOs is that the former are independent of state while NGOs are run by funding from national and international donors.

Civil society is not a modern phenomenon in the region. In fact, it is the traditional bodies which operate at the local level which have a direct relevance to the people. It can be said that civil society in the region can be understood in three broad ways. First, many of the local bodies are formed on primordial and kinship lines. Secondly, they are highly ethnically-based and so often exclusivist. Moreover, they are modern in the sense that many of the organisations are registered and operate under certain set of rules, norms and guidelines. In this way, one can say that the constituent units of the myriad organisations in the region fit in the understanding of civil society of the Western literature (Banerjee 2009).

Civil Society and Ethno-nationalism in the North-East India

North-East India as a region has continued to witness numerous ethno-nationalist movements. While much of the studies and writings about ethno-nationalist movements in the region tend to focus on the post-colonial era, many of them have their origin from the colonial period. In most of the ethnic political movements/assertions, it is the civil society that has often taken the leading role. To put it differently, civil society groups often lay the ground for ethnic assertions/ movements in both colonial and post-colonial India. It is also the case that in North-East India, many NGOs, philanthropic and/or ethnic-based civil society are often found to mediate between the state and the insurgent groups and between different ethnic groups themselves.

A very interesting aspect of the ethnic movements in the NE is the crucial role that the civil society plays. In most of the ethnic assertions, it was the civil society which formed the basis or the ground for such movements to take off. This is true for the case of the Nagas, Mizo (Zo people), Assamese, Bodos, etc. In fact, the formation of Naga Club was instrumental in sowing the seeds of the Naga nationalist movements. Civil society groups such as the United Naga Council (UNC), Naga People Movement for Human Rights (NPMHR) are openly supporting the cause of the Nagas. The objective of the NPMHR is "the right to live together as a people and the unification of all Naga lands". The UNC has been vocal in raising the demands for alternative arrangement of the Nagas in Manipur. In the case of Assam, the All Assam Students Union is at the forefront against the illegal migrants issue in Assam. The AASU provided the best leadership in this movement (Banerjee 2009: 163).

To supplement the arguments on civil society engagement with ethnic political assertions, we will take up the case of the Zo people in the discussion that follows.

Put under different administrative units from colonial period, the Zo people have demanded the integration of all the Zo inhabited areas. To make the matter worse, they are turned into minority in all the countries they live. The Zo political aspirations and struggle cannot be called as a "separatist" movement. Their demand is to re-unify the scattered Zos under one administration. It is in this framework that we will locate civil society engagement with ethnic political aspirations of the Zo people.

The struggle of the Zo people dates back to the colonial period, though a more organised struggle was launched in the post-colonial era at the levels of both armed and non-armed struggles. The first attempt at bringing the Zo people under one administration found its expression in the Chin-Lushai Conference of 1892. This Conference, held at Fort William, Calcutta on 29th January 1892, attempted to bring the Zos under one administration (Shyamkishore 2010: 135). One of the resolutions of the conference states, "The majority of the Conference are of opinion that it is very desirable that the whole tract of country known as Chin-Lushai Hills should be brought under one administrative head as soon as this can be done. They also consider it advisable that the new administration should be subordinate to the Chief Commissioner of Assam". Convened by the British, the conference is credited as the first serious attempt of the Zo people to find ways to bring about administrative and political unification to territories occupied by them and which are by now apportioned between the independent states of Bangladesh, India and Myanmar (Suan 2009). Yet, the only major outcome of the conference was the amalgamation of North and South Lushai Hills, while the major demands of the Zo people for the unification of their inhabited areas continue to remain unfulfilled and fall on deaf ears.

With the emergence of ethnic-based civil society in the post-Independent India, the Zo people witnessed the development of an organised struggle. It is here that civil society plays a key role. In spite of their internal differences and existence of many ethnic-based organisations, one can see the common political aspirations among them. That is, to re-unify all the Zos under one administration. In post-colonial India, the Zo people have put forward their objective of living under one nation under the banner of Mizo Union which demanded "territorial integrity and solidarity and self-determination" (Suan 2009: 272). On the same line, the Paite National Council (PNC) in 1960 submitted a memorandum to the Government of India and demanded "for a stable and sound administration of the country and as our legitimate rights, we for and on behalf of all the Chin people, put forth this demand for the re-unification of the Chins within one country where every community can have district or division or region for the preservation of their fundamental rights".

Although the movement continues, it was not until the formation of the Zo-Reunification Organisation (ZORO) in 1993, which brings back or revives the dream of the Zo people. The formation of ZORO was a historic moment for the Zo people and their struggle as it revived the hope and the aspirations of the Zo people once again. Under the aegis of ZORO, the First World Zomi Convention was held at Champhai in Mizoram from 19-21 May 1993. Though it went unnoticed by the Indian press, the Convention became the forerunner of Zo reunification with the avowed object of unifying the Indian state of Mizoram and the Chin state of Myanmar where the Zo descendants are predominant (Pau 2007: 187). The Convention reaffirmed their desire for integration by unanimously declaring, "We, the people of Zo ethnic groups, inhabitants of the highland in the Chin Hills and Arakans of Burma, the Chittagong Hill Tracts of Bangladesh, the state of Mizoram and adjoining hill areas of India, are descendants of one ancestor". What was significant about the Convention is that the Zo people met for the first time over an issue that they had long been airing separately (*Ibid*: 187). It was also from this Convention that ZORO was born, which till today continues to work tirelessly for the unification of the Zo people.

Re-unification of the Zo people and the regaining of the Zo national identity has been the top agenda of the ZORO. It submitted a memorandum to the United Nations on 20th May 1995 "seeking support and intervention of the UN by providing historical facts and appealing the UN to correct historical injustice meted out against these communities". The memorandum states, "Re-unification of the members of this family known today under various names and nomenclatures falls within the subject matters with which the Atlantic Charter and the objectives of the United Nations which are most concerned seriously". The organisation also continued to represent the Zo communities at the UN Permanent Forum on Indigenous Issues from 1999 onwards. The ZORO continues to work and stick to its principle of struggling and achieving its objectives through non-violent means.

The Zo people of India and elsewhere have been launching numerous struggles. For instance, under the banner of the Zomi Council, the Zos in Manipur submitted a memorandum to the Government of India in 2011. The memorandum demanded the creation of autonomous tribal state (ATS) in Manipur under the provision of Article 244 (A) of the Constitution of India. In the same manner, the Kuki Inpi Manipur (KIM) also demanded for a separate Kuki state. The involvement of ZC and KIM, two apex ethnic-based organisations of the Zos, in voicing the political aspirations of their people in Manipur clearly shows the crucial role played by civil society groups. In other words, civil societies in the North-East are taking part in the ethno-nationalist movements of the region. Many a times, they organised public demonstrations, strikes and other protests movement to achieve their objective. Since civil societies are working under the framework of the law as compared to the armed groups, they provide a scope for civilian participation. In this way, they have filled the gap which the armed groups could not fulfill.

Future Challenges: The Way Forward

The active participation or involvement of civil society of NE India in ethno-political assertion clearly reflects the ethnic nature of civil society in the region. Although this can have a positive contribution in many ways, it put the people and the region in a very disadvantaged position when looked from a larger socio-political perspective. In many instances, civil societies are caught in the ethnic trap which limits their legitimacy and relevance to their ethnic members only. Consequently, civil societies in the North-East are facing a number of challenges.

The existence of ethnic-based civil society in the NE is also an indication of the division of the different ethnic groups of the region along the ethnic lines. What this entails is that civil societies are very particular in the way they are operating. They often limit themselves to the cause of their ethnic groups. At times, they are involved in the very process of domination and subjugation. This issue of the ethnic character of civil society in the region has weakened the very civil society.

Subsequently, the very idea of "civility" and the voice represented by the civil society become an issue of great concern. As put by Patricia Mukhim (2010), "Till today, civil societies in our context are exclusive groups which do not believe in participatory decision building, but assume that their actions are endorsed by the silent majority". Therefore, civil societies in the NE are caught in the ethnic trap or ethnic politics. Often, they are engaged in opposing one another and prefer to take the undemocratic forms at many occasions. For example, human rights organisations in the region, said to believe in human rights, may not necessarily come out to raise their voice when the state and non-state actors are engaged in human rights violation against one ethnic group. In other words, as put by Phanjoubam (2009), "It is not uncommon to even hear of self-proclaimed human rights organisations speaking two different and mutually hostile languages on many issues". Civil society in the NE selectively condemns and protests as well.

Although it is highly positive that civil societies are engaging in ethno-national movements, this has put them in close relation to the armed groups itself. This clearly shows the undeniable fact of the relationship between civil society and armed groups. In the words of McDuie-Ra (2009), "It is very difficult to divorce civil society from insurgency as many of the insurgents were developed within political and cultural movements, and the actual level of association between the two is hard to establish". The result is not only a complication of the conflicts themselves, but also a discrediting of this very same "civil society" space, ultimately tarnishing the image of the civil society (Phanjoubam 2009: 69). The issue becomes more complicated looking at the obnoxious web of nexus between armed groups and politicians as well as the armed military forces. Thus, the civil society becomes trapped in the vicious cycle of conflicts and makes the notion of "civil society" vulnerable to be reduced to the status of mere tools of conflict.

Civil society in the North-East in many instances could not act as a mediator or change agent. This is because, in too many instances, civil society acts as the arm for carrying forward numerous exclusivist propagandas. An example can be taken of the United Naga Council serving "quit notice" to the Kuki inhabitants in four districts of Manipur in the early part of the 1990s. This has created an atmosphere of tension between the two communities, which later on spiralled into violent ethnic conflict. The Kuki-Naga conflict of 1992 has its roots in the quit notice served by the UNC. Civil society becomes an inseparable part of exclusivist agenda and their actions often take a violent turn as was in the case of Kuki-Naga conflict. Thus, when civil societies are found to engage in such activities, it consequently leads to the absence of space for dialogue among the different communities. The outcome to this is that the effectiveness of civil society is put at stake and further jeopardised due to this.

The challenge that lies ahead is, therefore, building a new democratic space where a true civil participation can take place. Not only this, in a multi-ethnic region like the NE, it is pertinent to follow the principles of accommodation and a space for dialogue between different ethnic communities. Such space at present is absent and as long as the people of the region acknowledge the differences and come together, it will be a dream to achieve actual democratisation. This space for dialogue is crucial to strengthen, rejuvenate and re-invent their very self-determination struggles as well. It is an utmost necessity that civil society of the region should reform and transform itself. As put by Das (2009), "If civil society is posited as a solution, then we certainly need to reform it". This reformation will have to earmark a new beginning for the region and for the people.

Conclusion

It is understandable that civil societies in the North-East are heavily ethnicised. The nature and operations of the civil societies often are limited to their ethnic groups only. More importantly, they are directly engaging in the ethnic aspirations of their respective communities and many of them are spearheading such movements. This makes conceptualisation and theoretical understanding of civil society in the NE a challenging task for scholars and academicians. However, it may be a danger to say that there is no civil society in the region.

At another level, civil societies in the NE are not only "sites of conflicts" but also "sites of negotiations". In many instances, it is the civil societies who are playing the catalystic role for bringing about peace and tranquility in the region. Even though the civil societies are engaged in the ethnic politics of the region, it is they who are important agent in transforming the region by setting common agenda. In a conflict ridden region like the NE, civil society is the space where the major public at large can raise their voice and demand their democratic rights. Civil society can fill two important gaps. First is the "trust deficit" among different ethnic communities, and second is the "democratic deficit" by giving the principles of accommodation a priority. The future course of politics in the NE largely lies at the hands of the civil societies which will depend on their capability in transforming themselves and then the region.

Notes

1. The Zo people today are identified by different names such as Chin, Mizo, Kuki, Zomi. They are dispersed in three different countries viz., India, Bangladesh and Myanmar.
2. The Zo inhabited areas cut across three states of India (Manipur, Mizoram and Tripura), the Chin Hills in Burma and parts of Chittagong Hill Tracts (CHTs) in Bangladesh.

References

2012: "1993: First World Zomi Convention", available at *http://www.zogam.org/documents.asp?article=documents_213,* viewed on 2nd January 2012.

2012: "Memorandum submitted by the Paite National Council (PNC) to the Prime Minister of India", Government of India, 1960, available at *http://www.zogam.org/documents.asp?article=documents_242,* viewed on 3rd November 2013.

Banerjee, M (2009): "Civil Society and Violence in India's North-East", *Journal of Civil Society,* 5(2): 151-167.

Baruah, S (2010): *Ethnonationalism in India: A Reader* (New Delhi: Oxford University Press).

Beteille, A (2001): "Civil Society and the Good Society", *Sociological Bulletin,* 50(2): 286-307.

Carothers, T and Barndt, W (1999-2000): "Civil Society", *Foreign Policy,* 117: 18-29.

Chandhoke, N (1995): *State and Civil Society: Considerations in Political Theory* (New Delhi: Sage Publications).

Chandhoke, N (2007): "Civil Society", *Development in Practice,* 17(4/5): 607-614.

Das, SK (2007): *Conflict and Peace in India's North-East: The Role of Civil Society,* Policy Studies 42, East-West Center Organisation.

Das, SK (2009): "Land, Identity and Conflicts: A Plea for Rebuilding Civil Society in North-East", in P Singh (ed.), *Tribalism and the Tragedy of the Commons: Land, Identity and Development the Manipur Experience* (New Delhi: Akansha Publishing House).

Dhanagare, DN (2001): "Civil Society, State and Democracy: Contextualising a Discourse", *Sociological Bulletin,* 50(2): 167-191.

Jayaram, N (2005): "An Introduction to the Discourse", in N Jayaram (ed.), *On Civil Society: Issues and Perspectives* (New Delhi: Sage Publications).

Kaitz, H (2006): "Gramsci, Hegemony, and Global Civil Society Network", *International Journal of Voluntary and Non-profit Organisations,* 17 (4): 333-348.

Kham Khan Suan, H (2009): "Hills-Valley Divide as a Site of Conflict: Emerging Dialogic Space in Manipur", in S Baruah (ed.), *Beyond Counter-insurgency: Breaking the Impasse in North-East India* (New Delhi: Oxford University Press).

Kham Khan Suan, H (2011): "Rethinking 'Tribe' Identities: The Politics of Recognition Among the Zo in North-East India", *Contributions to Indian Sociology,* 45(2): 157-187.

Khilani, S (2001): "The Development of Civil Society", in S Kaviraj and S Khilani (ed.), *Civil Society: History and Possibilities* (New Delhi: Cambridge University Press).

Mahanta, NG (2007): "Ethnicity, State and Identity: From Confrontation to Co-existence in Problems of Ethnicity in North-East India", in B B Kumar (ed.), *Problems of Ethnicity in North-East India* (New Delhi: Concept Publishing Company).

McDuie-Ra, Duncan (2007): "Civil Society Organisations and Human Security: Transcending Constricted Space in Meghalaya", *Contemporary South Asia,* 15 (1): 35-53.

McDuie-Ra, Duncan (2009): Civil *Society, Democratisation and the Search for Human Security: The Politics of the Environment, Gender, and Identity in North-East India* (New York: Nova Science Publishers).

Mukhim, Patricia (2010): "Civil Society in India's North-East: Can it Still Help resolve Conflict in the Region?", in W Hussain (ed.), *Peace, Tools and Conflict Nuances in India's North-East* (Guwahati: Wordweaves India).

Pau, Pum Khan (2007): "Administrative Rivalries on a Frontier: Problem of the Chin-Lushai Hills", *Indian Historical Review,* 34: 187-209.

Phanjoubam, P (2009): "Fragmented Civil Society: Problems and Prospects", in P Singh (ed.), *Tribalism and the Tragedy of the Commons: Land, Identity and Development the Manipur Experience* (New Delhi: Akansha Publishing House).

Shyamkishore, A (2010): "In Search of Common Identity: A Study of Chin-Kuki-Mizo Community in India", *International Journal of South Asian Studies,* 3(1): 131-139.

Tandon, R (2003): "The Civil Society-governance Interface: An Indian Perspective", in R Tandon and R Mohanty (ed.), *Does Civil Society Matter: Governance in Contemporary India* (New Delhi: Sage Publications).

Ulhin, A (2009): "Which Characteristics of Civil Society Organisations Support What Aspects of Democracy? Evidence from Post-communist Latvia", *International Political Science Review*, 30(2): 271-295.

UNC (2011): "The Movement for Alternative Arrangement for the Nagas in Manipur", the United Naga Council (UNC).

Zou, David Vumlallian (2010): "A Historical Study of the 'Zo' Struggle", *Economic and Political Weekly*, 45(14): 56-63.

10

State, Tribe and Democracy

(The Zomi Cause)

H. Kamkhenthang **and** ***Asok Kumar Ray***

Identity of the Zomis

The Zomis are encapsulated in the larger cluster of Chin-Kuki linguistic group in Manipur. Zoumi or Zomi (Mizo) is a generic term for people who were called either Chin or Kuki since the British period or even earlier in undivided India and Burma. They are found in the states of Mizoram and Manipur in India; Chin state of Myanmar; Jampui and Sakhan range (Tripura); hill tracts of Chittagong (Bangladesh), Arakan (Burma), upper and lower areas of Chindwin River. The term *"Zo"* or Zomi had been in use to mean the Chin-Kuki linguistic group of people excluding the Meiteis (Manipuris). It is an archaic poetical word. The term *"Zo"* had been in use since time immemorial in poetical parlance and it remained buried in dormancy in socio-cultural layers.

Zomi is a style of writing adopted in the former Lushai hills. This style of writing is confusing to many as it may be read as Zawmi (in long sound) when the "o" in Zomi is not made to have a sound of "ou". The Mizo style of "o" sounds as "ou" in writing it as Zomi. Phonologically, it is more correct to write *"Zo"* or Zomi as Zou or Zoumi as it is nearer to international phonetic sound than the conventional writing introduced by missionaries in the Chin hills and Lushai hills more than one hundred years back.

We are following, provisionally for this paper, the "o" style. That is, Zou as Zo and Mizou and Zoumi as Mizo and Zomi, respectively, as majority follow the style as (process of) democracy is determined by number but not necessarily by qualitative consideration.

Poetical use of the term indicating its remoteness may be seen in the following poetical phrases. The poetic word for cold water of the hills is *"zodam siktui"* and *"zodam huihkhi"* is the poetic word for cold breeze of the hills. The hilly cultivation field is called *"zolou"*. It is assumed that *"Zo"* was the eponymous ancestor of the Zo people and his progenies are Zomi (Mizo). There are several groups of people known by a name *"Zo"*, either prefixed or not prefixed with the term *"Zo"* or written to mean *"Zo"* as *"yo"*, *Sho, Jo* or *Dzo, sho, Zomi, Mizo, Laimi,* etc., who are all very closed cognates to one another. The soil of the earth on which the people cultivate is called *"Zolei"*. The land they live in is *"Zogam/Zoram"* and the range of hills is *"zotlang"*. The vast stretch of land to a poet is *"Zokuam"*. A song composed by Kamkhenthang clearly shows it all. The original wording of the song is appended herewith for better understanding of the complicacy of the song.

Pupa gam satsa,

Gam zilza sakmin ngaih;

Thei bang lohna Zogam,

Zomite'n khuam bang luah.

Zodam huihkhi leh/Zodam siktui a;

Limnga bang bualte/Zomi hi hang e.

Zodam siktui siang/Zaitha tawl hehnepna;

Damsiktui lung dimdim,

Zodam siktui hi e.

Zogam kuam zilza,

Mualchin sang huihkhi lang;

Pupa sakmin lohna,

Zodam huihkhi hi e.

[Translation]:

The land founded by forefathers,

Sprawling vast land

By the name Zogam

Occupy by the Zomi.

The cold breeze (zodam huihkhi)/The cold waters of hills (zodam siktui)

Those that wallow as fish therein/Are all Zomi

The cold water called zodam siktui/A refresher for those who toil hard

The water flows rippling

The sprawling vast land of Zogam

Every hills is windy and cold

Forefathers called it zodam huihkhi

By the name zodam huihkhi (cold breeze of the high hills)

It is called zodam siktui.

Democratic Elements in Zomi Political System

Vumson found the clan system of the *"Zo"* that constituted a village which was an independent unit. He stated that the southern Zos shifted village in a circular or repeating pattern whereas the northern people moved further and further north and west. The people of the central Zo country were less migratory than those of the northern and southern. Each village had a chief or a headman. Hereditary chieftainship was common in the northern part of the country, whereas in the southern part, a headman or a village leader ruled the village. In some instances, a chief would rule over several villages. The chief was responsible for land division, disposal, sequestration and redistribution within the village boundary. In the northern Zo country, the headman would collect tax or dues for the chief.

In the southern Zo country where no *"matu"* (chief) arose, the headman or the village leader would lend his name to the village and he was assisted by his councilors. Although the chief usually owned the land, there were chiefs who did not completely own land. In the Sizang area, the chief and the commoners each owned their own fields. Vumson wrote that at the time when British conquered, the Zo people of Falam had developed itself into the most powerful of the chieftainships in Zo country. But the Falam people integrated all peoples equally and without prejudice. Thus, the Falams were not only powerful but enjoyed the trust of most of the Zo people from the Lushai hills to the Burmese border. Vumson further wrote that they might one day have united all Zo people had not the British appeared on the scene. Even today, the Falams are not clannish and a newcomer to Falam is accepted as one of them so that the Falam is the most pleasant in the whole Zo area.

The overall social structure of Zo was communal (communism). They have always practised a form of socialism within their communities. This form of socialism is called *"tlawmngaihna"* in Lushai dialect, which means, "love of less" and which Samuelson explained as the capacity for hard work, bravery, endurance, generosity, kindness and selfishness. The concept of *"tlawmngaihna"* was a stabilising force (Vumson 1987).

Though the colonial rulers categorised the Zo political system as authoritarian, many elements of incipient democracy in the tribe was not captured in right spirit. Some of these are:

Non-accumulative Economy of the Zomis

The Zomis practised shifting cultivation which was not based on accumulative economy. Even though the Zomi chiefs were the virtual owners of the land, their ownership was not akin to the Zamindari or *ryotwari* system as in the valley areas of other parts of India. In fact, the chief is *de facto* and *de jure* owner of his village and the village land. Their ownership was only notional. Originally, the chiefs kept the land under their control to keep solidarity among the community members. There was no sense of personal accumulation except that the chiefs required the villagers to cultivate his land. The villagers in turn gave an annual payment of paddy and one scapular part of four-footed wild animal killed in the village land of the chief as tribute to the chiefs.

These customary tributes did not lead to surplus accumulation. The village and the chieftainship organisation were held in high esteem by both the community and the chief. Thus for knowing the identity of a person, the usual manner of asking was, *"Nang kua khua na hiam?"* It literally means, to whose village you belong. In response to this, the person was to mention the name of the village, and sometimes the name of the village chief with the name of the village. The chiefs had traditional rights over their lands even before the British colonial administrators amalgamated their lands to Manipur. In the Lushai hills, the chieftainship institution was abolished by the then Assam Government by an Act in 1954 on paying compensation to them.

In Manipur, the situation was complicated. Although the State government passed the Manipur Hill Areas (Acquisition of Chieftainship Right) Act in 1967, it was not implemented till date. On the other hand, on accession of Manipur to the Union of India, the Meitei king was given privy purse like the other kings and rulers of the native states. By introducing the MLR and LR Act, 1960, the State government of Manipur knowingly ignored the chiefs' rights. All these created suspicion in the minds of the hill people. Many problems were created by the extension of the Act in the hill areas in Manipur. The Law Research Institute of Eastern Region, Gauhati High Court, observed the ignoring of the rights of the chiefs by the Government of Manipur as follows:

> "But how could the chiefs' rights over land be ignored? The rights have not yet been acquired by the government. A legislation for the acquisition of chiefs' rights, called Manipur Hill Areas (Acquisition of Chief's Rights) Act, 1976, has been enacted but it has not been implemented yet. In Mizoram, similar legislation, called the Assam Lushai Hills District (Acquisition of Chiefs' Rights) Act 1964, had been passed long ago and was forthwith implemented. The Mizo chiefs who had enjoyed the same kind of rights over the village land as the Kuki chiefs do now in Manipur has disappeared and the Mizoram Government has now issued *pattas* to the erstwhile tenants of the Mizo chiefs. This should have been and may still be the model for Manipur fringe-villages to which the MLR and LR Act 1960 has been extended" (Das 1989: 146).

Under the *jhum* economy, as per customary law, the chiefs allotted lands to the villagers for cultivation. In other words, trustees of the *jhum* land were traditionally under the discretionary power of the chief. No individual was allowed to transfer land to the outsiders except the chief. This kept up the social, cultural as well as economic bond among the people. Their identity, cultural practices and their social bonds were all built around customary land holding system. The system of community labour in shifting cultivation gave them a sense of social and cultural bond. Besides, the villagers enjoyed many rights under the rule of the chief. Right to free movement within the village territory, right to hunting and gathering from the forest for house construction, food, fodder and daily needs built an ideal environment for a communitarian society. Customary law allowed no transaction of forest products for commercial use. The villagers had right to cultivate the land as per the conditions laid down by the chief.

The concept of individual right, as we understand in the liberal constitution, did not apply to the shifting cultivators because of the non-sedentary nature of the economy. As regards to the system of land use, the concerned chief with his council of elders (authority) would decide the area, direction, etc., and the annual jhuming sites of the village land from year to year. After one *jhum* cycle was over, the chief might re-allocate the land in different manner. In every Zo village, the chief kept some village areas as village commons for community centre, village playground, religious worship and so on. The cultivation right of the subjects was protected through the instrument of the institution of chieftainship so that no villager was to face the problem of dispossession and alienation unless and until a person develops enmity with the chief. In case a man had serious disputes with the village chief, the latter could expel the former from his village. In such a case, the recalcitrant subject had to seek permission of settlement from another chief.

Justice Dispensing System of Zomis

The Zomis had a non-adversarial justice system. In their justice dispensing system, there was no capital punishment to a serious offender. In case of serious offense, the maximum punishment was fine of different degrees or ex-communication. As the head and guardian of the tribe, the chief had greater responsibility to maintain group cohesion and integrity of the people. Though he received some tributary privileges like hind leg of slain wild animal and basketful of paddy, this was not tax or forceful collection. The customary privileges and rights provided legitimacy to his powers and authority.

The chief worked with a team of village council and the traditional custom required the chief to appoint the elders to assist him in administration of the village. There was no room for command that the chief might proclaim. He was always expected to have a team of elders/councilors who were expert and well-versed in traditional customs and rules. The selection and distribution of land to the people was done by the chief in consultation with the elders, although the chief and members of the council first got the most fertile land for cultivation.

In the Zomi society, we found no clear distinction between social and political role of the chiefs. While they were political heads of the tribe, they also had a lot of responsibilities in social matters. The non-adversarial justice system has the added advantage of promoting customary law and traditions, of reducing ill-will, of easy approachability, of early settlement at low costs. In fact, the concept of non-adversarial justice seems to have grown out of the great body of customary law and seems to follow a pattern worldwide (Goswami 2010).

The chief has the right to accept or to refuse a new family to settle in his village or within any part of the village territory. Without his permission, no one can migrate into his village. Under normal circumstances, the village chief is not to refuse allotting a plot of land for *jhum* cultivation year after year. He can confiscate the property of a person who earned his displeasure. Confiscating properties of a villager, called *"innkhak-loukhak"*, includes the paddy and the house of a recalcitrant villager. For the betterment of the village community, the chief imposes certain restrictions. Burning of forest, felling of trees in the village reserved forest invites penalty in the form of fines. One case of severe form of penalty goes as follows. There was an old widower living alone in poverty. He wanted a standing dried tree for firewood. He could not cut it. He had to fell it and burn it at the base. The fire spread around and burnt the forest. The chief imposed a punitive fine of a pig. His men caught the pig for a punitive feast. The old man could not bear the thought and he committed suicide by hanging himself.

Social Democracy

At the social front, absence of caste hierarchy was a great boon. In fact, they are an open society having no effect of casteism like the Burmans. Unlike the other parts of India, the Zomi society was gender balanced and men-women relations were binary. They practise equal food sharing among all the family members, including the women, and consumption of food together gives a sense of strong family bond. In the social democracy, the women have no equal rights and opportunities with the men. At the moment of birth after parturition, it is inquired whether the new born is a stranger or a local, meaning whether the child is a girl or a boy. There is no discrimination between male and female children in Zomi society. Although women have no real voice in the *"Inndongta"* (household council), they are the main pillar of the household.

Customarily, the women had no right to inheritance of property. But a beginning has been made for the improvement of the lot of women by the Paite Tribe Council (one of the constituent tribes of the Zomi) making a provision for inheritance of woman who has neither uterine brother nor half brother. Men and women have clear-cut division of labour and role along the line of biological differences. There are situations of conflation of new and the old practices, where the norm of social democracy starts working. The ritual transformation of the people from their original belief to Christianity strengthened the process of democratic awareness about parliamentary democracy. This factor made many women of the Zomis to fight for their democratic rights and to find a place in the women societies, student bodies, and so on.

In the custom, a woman is supposed to be restrained in her behaviour, action and speech and a man dislikes to be dictated by his wife. A clear illustration is seen in a folk story which goes—a family had to kill a pig for a feast. He gingerly approached the pig from behind to catch it by the hind legs. In the meantime, his wife said and asked him unnecessarily to catch the pig by the hind legs. He felt her verbal intervention uncalled for. He suddenly caught the pig by one of the fore legs. The pig was too strong to be held by one of its fore legs. He undid his hand grip and the pig escaped. But in the changing circumstances, the women came to assume greater role in household decision-making process and the male members give due respect and weightage to her role.

Community worship and ritual sacrifice for collective welfare and group work in the *jhum* field are some more features of social democracy. The chief also is to look after the poor and widows in the village and exempt them from public or communal works and condone payment of annual rent of paddy to some persons. He also shares the sufferings of others that is captured in a folk saying—Whenever a foreign body enters the eye of a child, the mother or grandmother opens the affected eye and blows it and saying, let the foreign body enter the eye of the chief. This is believed to relieve the child. That was how he came to command a great respect from the people.

For the spiritual welfare of the people, the chiefs also arrange annual community worship through the ritual expert, called *"siampu"*, who run the whole process of community sacrifice on annual basis. This is done for the good physical and spiritual health of the people, successful hunting and for abundant harvest. At the end of the season, a harvest festival, called *"Khuadou"*, is performed. The village chief can appoint the ritual expert to exorcise evil spirits through ritual offerings for good health and the village blacksmith is to prepare tools for the agriculture purpose. These functionaries have the privilege of collecting small quantity of paddy for their service to the public as arranged by the chief. The village crier makes announcement to the public for these rituals. The importance of these officials to the village chief in running the village affairs is often compared with the importance of a tripod oven which the Zomi community requires in the daily domestic life.

Haam—the Bachelor's Dormitory

By tradition, it was mandatory on all tribal youths over age puberty to stay in "bachelor's dormitories". It was in this social institution that the youth received training in tribal warfare, wrestling, hunting, folklore and village government. The training was intensive and strenuous, strict discipline was maintained, and basic values of life were inculcated into the youngsters. In other words, the "bachelor dormitory" was an institution where the young tribal males not only picked up skills in self-defence but also developed a positive attitude to life based on hope-spun values as well (Sanga 2012).

Right to Desert the Autocratic Chief

People could desert an autocratic chief for excess or misuse of power. This acted as auto-limitation to the chief's power. The chief could not ordinarily deny any villager the right to cultivate the land either. As per the custom, there was no scope for the chief to act as an autocrat. Moreover, the social role of youth dormitories needed be reckoned with. The chief could also donate land to government for construction of primary health centres, schools and for other public purposes. Any encroachment in the village commons was prohibited and liable to punishment. A village common remained under the direct control of the chief and the members of the village community. The homestead land was vested in the village community and the chief gave each household a plot of land for house construction. In order to maintain unity and discipline in the community, the chief, as the guardian of the village, might turn out the recalcitrant villager from the village and confiscate his properties.

The Colonial Phase

The colonial rulers occupied the hills inhabited by the Zos and made efforts to bring them under the administrative control of the British. After the Lushai Expedition, the "Chin-Lushai Conference" became a landmark in the Zos history. This Conference was organised by the British officers at Calcutta on 29th January 1892, which resolved to bring the Chin-Lushai hills tract under one administrative head as soon as it could be done, and to construct communications for administrative convenience and boundary demarcation of the tract to bring it under the British control. These resolutions were kept pending till there was military capture of a portion of Zomi country and formal declaration was made on probation that the part of the said territory should be under the lower provinces of Assam, Bengal and Burma on

6th September 1895. However, rules and regulations applied to those provinces were not applied in the Zo country. On the same day, they applied the Scheduled District Act 1874.

The Chin-Lushai-Kuki territory was brought under the Bengal Eastern Frontier Regulation Acts 1873 in 1875. However, the Chin Hills Regulation 1896 was not applied to the Zomi territories as these did not yet come under single administrative unit. In 1898; following the Conference resolution, a part of Southern Lushai hills and Arakan hills was brought under the Schedule District Act, although the resolution to bring the Chin-Lushai hills tract under one administrative head was kept pending. In 1904, the Assam Frontier Tract Regulation 1880 was applied to Zomi territories and the Chin Hills Regulation 1896 was extended to the Zo country in 1911.

In the context of political unrest in India after 1920, the Zo country was further protected and the entry of the hill tribes into the plain areas was reversed and the entry of the plain people into the tribal areas was restricted on 28th July 1930. The Government of India Act 1935 promulgating the "Excluded" and "Partially Excluded Areas" was extended to Zomi country in 1936. The colonial intervention brought changes in the nature of the Zomi chieftainship system. Many of the pre-colonial features of the chieftainship institution were lost. It is from the colonial times onward that some of the chiefs were patronised to play instrumental roles in favour of the British and the primary allegiance of such chiefs shifted from the community towards the colonial masters. The leadership role of the Zo chiefs was instrumentalised by the colonial rulers to use them as buffers.

Induction to Procedural Democracy

The Westphalian template of republicanism built the radical imagination of democracy based on nation-state conflation, constitutional freedom, election and adult-franchise, individualism, etc. Procedural democracy was established as the universal and standardised model, which reduced the broader spectrum of democracy incipient in the Zomi tribe. Procedural democracy captured the administrators, anthropologists and the social scientists to categorise the political system of the Zomi tribe as authoritarian through the lens of the state-constructed democracy. On the other hand, in the tribal society, the democracy was more an ontological product than a state construct that worked as marker of common identity and collective consciousness and at the same time built the complementarity (complementing each other) between the political and the social. While the project of democracy of the Indian state had the objective of structural transformation of the Indian society through political democracy, in the tribal society the elements of libertarianism were already present. This created a thorough gap in understanding the tribal political systems and the nature of Indian democracy. From the very beginning of Indian independence, the polarity between the state-nation and the ethnic-nation surfaced in the Zomi society. The Indian state, however, promoted a kind of pan Indianism that did not match with the ethnic nationalist aspirations. There were a number of instruments for the induction of procedural democracy through which the tribal people could be integrated in the larger Indian state.

There were a few criticalities in the process of democratisation of the Indian polity. First, in India, the state formation process preceded the nation formation. The ethnic nationhood of the Zomis or, for that matter, that of the entire tribal world, was taken to be subsumed within the larger Indian nationhood dream. Secondly, the territorial boundary of the Indian state cut across the ethnic boundaries. Thirdly, in place of mainstreaming, there was state-ethnic enclavisation in which the Zomi tribe was trapped. Fourthly, as a consequence, space became a contesting playing field of the state and the ethnic. Given these criticalities, some of the legal and regulatory instruments, relevant to the Zomis in India, were discussed below.

Manipur State Hill People Regulation 1947

This regulation transferred the hill administration from the Manipur state Darbar to the Maharaja of Manipur and was to be exercised in accordance with the constitution act of the state and provisions of this Regulation. The suggestions of the Maharaja of Manipur to amend and modify the regulation (mainly on forced labour) were taken up. This regulation brought new authority structure and new institutions on paper. The regulation required that in each village of 20 tax-paying houses or over, there shall be constituted a village authority which shall be nominated in accordance with the custom of the village and shall consist of the chief or *"khullakpa"* of the village with his council of elders, if any. The village authority so nominated shall be formally recognised by the sub-divisional officer who shall be final authority in matters concerning appointment and constitution of village authority saving that an appeal shall lie in the minister-in-charge of hill administration from the decision of any sub-divisional officer in such matters. For the purpose of administration of all villages, to which this regulation applied, they were grouped into circles and sub-divisions.

Village Authorities in the Hill Areas Act 1956

Under this Act, the chiefs were legally dethroned from their political functions and the absolute power of the chieftainship institution degraded considerably in the hill areas of Manipur. The new village authority under the new Act did not and could not function. Instead of strengthening the system of administration, it rather thwarted, according to the letter as the Act contained provisions which were not suitable. As such, the Village Authority Act, 1956 and the Manipur (Hill Areas District Council) Act 1971 are currently under scanning of the expert committee. Under the Village Authority Act, each revenue village is vested in a new council with members directly elected by the people on the basis of adult franchise with the chief as the ex-officio chairman. All matters including land were to be decided by the elected village authority.

Despite political changes and new administrative set-up democratically formed, the Zo chief's role was not completely eliminated. The traditional authorities of the chiefs are still accepted as legitimate in the eyes of a large section of people. The chief acting as ex-officio chairman of the village authority interprets and administers customary laws. Abolition of chieftainship among the Zos has not been possible because of its symbolic value. However, the customary dues payable to the chiefs by the villagers have been discontinued with the introduction of the village authorities in the hill areas. But many village chiefs regained their rights to prerogative annual collection in acknowledgement of the rights of the chiefs as the owners of the land. It is to be noted that this Act faced stiff opposition from the Zo chiefs in the early 1970s.

Manipur Hill Areas (Acquisition of Chieftainship Right) Act 1967

Unlike Mizoram, this Act, passed on 10th January 1967 in Manipur, could not be brought into operation due to local resistance. On the other hand, acquisition of chieftainship right had already started in Assam in 1954. By the Assam Lushai Hills District (Acquisition of Chiefs Right) Act, 1954, the rights and interests of 259 Mizo chiefs and 50 Pawi Lakher chiefs were vested in the government. The motive force behind this Act was the Mizo Union (MU) that led the movement against abolition of the Mizo chieftains and illegal extraction practices by them. The MU boycotted the chiefs through a non-violent movement and instructed the villagers to stop payment of taxes to them. The government was made a party on the ground that it was supporting the authority of the chiefs. The people were urged to defy the authority of the government as well as of the chiefs and to join together in a full-scale civil disobedience movement. In the south district of Manipur, especially the Paites and the Lushais stopped payment of customary dues to the chiefs. Some people branded the chiefs as "hated despot" who suck the blood of the villagers by collecting *"buhsun and sating"* (Zathang 1982: 45).

The Manipur (Hill Areas District Council) Act

This Act was passed as an independent Act by the Indian Parliament in 1971, and the District Council Election Rules in 1972. The historical background of the enactment of this Act is reflected in the introductory statement issued by D.G. Bhave, special officer (reorganisation), on 14th March 1972. It says:

> "When the preparation for inauguration of statehood began in December 1971, the Lt. Governor, Mr. D.R. Kohli, had directed that simultaneous preparatory work for the establishment of district council should also be taken up. After the state was inaugurated on 21/1/72, I handed over as chief secretary on 31-1-72. The government appointed me to draft the necessary rules and initiate preliminary step for the establishment of the district councils. With the approval of the Governor, Mr. B.K. Nehru, I was directed to complete the initial work according to a time schedule. I am gratified that this could be done with the whole-hearted cooperation extended by the chief secretary, the secretaries to the government, deputy commissioners and other field officers".

The Manipur (Hill Areas District Council) Act was not equivalent to the Sixth Schedule of the Indian Constitution. Under the provision of the Sixth Schedule, the district council has power to make laws with respect to the allotment, occupation or use, or the setting apart of land, other than any land which is a reserved forest, for the purpose of agriculture or grazing or for residential or other non-agricultural purposes likely to promote the interests of the inhabitants of any village or town: Provided that nothing in such laws shall prevent the compulsory acquisition of any land, whether occupied or un-occupied, for public purposes by the government of the state concerned in accordance with the law for the time being in force authorising such acquisition; the management of any forest not being a reserved forest; the regulation of the practice of *jhum* or other forms of shifting cultivation; the establishment of village or town committees or councils and their powers; the inheritance of property, etc.

The powers and functions of the district council in Manipur were not similar to those of the Sixth Schedule. The State government still wants to tantalise its trans-frontier tribes by denying positive reply to the Government of India. All Tribal Students Union of Manipur became instrumental in the struggle for bringing the Sixth Schedule in the hill areas of Manipur. The first district council election across the hills was held in 1973. The second election was held in 1978, and the third election was held in 1983. The mid-term election in Senapati district council was held in 1988, and its term continued upto 1993. After a long gap of 20 years, election to the district council was held in 2010. During this intervening period, there was no proposal for election from all sides.

The Manipur Village Authority (in Hill Areas) Act, 1956

This Act was passed for the administration of the hill areas in the state of Manipur. The Act was implemented in 1957, determined the number of members of a village authority on the basis of the number of tax-paying houses. This Act may be regarded as one of the first steps towards the democratisation of hill administration in Manipur. By placing certain restrictions on the powers of the chief and by introducing adult franchise at the lowest level of administration, i.e., the village authority, the common villagers became aware of democratic values and practices. But the Act has certain elements of restricting certain customary practices. Zomi tribes in Manipur have their own 'kangaroo court' in common and people prefer Zomi court or Zomi Council or *"Inndongta"* (household council) for settlement of disputes in a customary way.

Electoral Democracy and the Clash

Electoral democracy, through which the elected members of the State Legislative Assembly or the Indian Parliament would represent the tribal interests, was numerically restricted for the Zomis. Education and awareness of the ordinary people has, however, increased and the nature of political participa-tion changed in course of time. The student communities, Church and civil organisations in the Zomi society are now organised on democratic platforms and have created space for democratic discourse. This has paved the alternative trajectory of democratisation in the Zomi society.

Despite these openings, the ethnic democratic movements in the post-Independence India had multitudinous self-determination plans appeared out of the deep dissatisfaction with the development projects concentrated either in the metropolitan pockets or in the ethnic spaces with abundance of raw materials and cheap labour. This problematised democracy and national integration. Roy Burman examined the problem of national integration at conceptual and empirical levels. His conceptual level was guided by certain variables like the ethical basis, linguistic-cultural relations, diversity, infra and proto nationalism in the nation-building process. His empirical level needed to be understood in the perspective of colonisation, independence movement, and the social movements. He critiqued the civilisational and cultural integration in India and the orthogenetic development of civilisation from a pre-mature cultural level based on evolutionary scheme that is independent of external factors (Sanskritisation). He found the infra and protonationalism marking a phase of expansion (small loyalty). The symbol of nation, after independence, was surcharged with power that gave rise to subordination of the minorities and some other sections of the society and let loose competition for the scare resources.

But the sociological factors in colonial India and the traditional settlement of national society were based on symbols of various segments that, without the backing of state power, did not mean much for domination of one over the other. In the post-colonial situation, minoritisation of certain communities bred subordination and frustration (Chakraborti and Basu 2012). This pluralisation posed challenge both to the methodological nationalism and the procedural democracy.

The internal dynamics of the Zomis was significant. From the very beginning, they started to mobilise their community for unification and Zomi National Congress (ZNC) was formed as a platform of the Zomis through which they could ventilate their grievances and aspirations. The Zomi reunification movement had veto chapter, viz., the Burma chapter and the India chapter. The Zomi had been reduced to the minority wherever they are after their inhabited areas were trifurcated as parts of India, Burma and Bangladesh. The independence of these countries instrumentally gripped, controlled, and trammeled and neglected the Zos in all aspects. They feel that they have no sufficient room to grow according to their genius.

Segments of certain hill areas of Zo settlements had been brought within the imaginary boundaries of British territory by the British officers. There had been regular Chin Regiments and Chin Rifles that provided a good opportunity of employments for the Zomi youths of India and Myanmar during the period from the British rule (in the undivided India and Burma to the beginning of Military rule in Burma). But the revolutionary military rulers of Burma systematically dismantled the two armed forces by scattering the personnel of the two forces in different forces of the Burma Army, thereby liquidating the Chin Regiments and the Chin Rifles. Countries having dispersed tribal population by means of euphemism used to publicise that the minority population and the major group lived together for thousands of years sharing their joys and sorrows as shown in the new Constitution of military ruled Burma. This kind of euphemism is an eyewash to the Zomi wherever they were reduced as neglected minorities. Their grievances are galore everywhere and the number of Zomi re-unification movements multiple in non-violence whereas the movements of other trans-frontier people like the Shan, Kachin, Karen are violent in their attempt to build their nationalism.

Zomi Re-unification Movement: The Burma Chapter

Tripartite division of the Zos deprived the Zo movement for the re-unification and self-determination. The re-unification movement of the Zos took a start from the disillusionment of the Panglong Agreement 1947. The Zo leaders from Tedim, Falam, Haka, Matupi, Mindat and Paletwa districts resolved to unite the six districts as Chin special division and to adopt 20th February as Zomi national day. This day is now observed as integration day by the Zomis in Burma and Manipur. They demanded freedom of Zoland (Chinland) by seceding from the Union of Burma as per Section 201-204 of the Constitution of Burma (1947). In this movement, the youth of the Shan state of Burma got involved and they led armed rebellion for secession. The first Constitution of Burma, however, created a special division of Zomi dominated areas comprising the Chin Hills district and Arakan hill tracts and created ministry of Chin affairs. But the economic and social development of the Zomis remained neglected. Imposition of Burmese language as the national language, and Buddhism as the state religion neglected the culture, history and languages of the Zo people. Burman domination over the Zo people, resource exploitation from the Zo country, neglect of Chin Hills, discrimination of the Zos in the Burmese army betrayed, deceived and thwarted the Zo community in Burma.

The Zomi Union's proposal for change of name from "Chin Hills" to "Zomi State" was rejected in the new Burmese Constitution of 1973. The Burmese state suppressed the democratic movement of the Zomis and their alignment with the Chin Liberation Army (CLA) in the early 1970's. The Burmese army also crushed the early bid for freedom by the CLA. Mistrust towards the oppressive Burmese regime, doubtful respect shown by the Burmese state towards the culture, language and belief system of the Zomis and their squeezed social space in Burma provoked them to lead mass movement for pan-Zo unification.

In the mid-1960's, Chin National Organisation (CNO) movement was short-lived. Two movements for re-unification, one led by ex-Lieutenant Colonel Son Kho Pau, Dam Kho Hau, Mangkhanpau and Tunkhopum, who mobilised support from the radical Zo leaders from Manipur and Mizoram and the other under the banner of the CLA that received support from some Paite leaders also faced setback. The next move of the Zomis to align with the Mizo National Front also did not materialise and finally the re-unification movement remained the cherished dreams of the Zo leaders.

The waves of the Zomi unification movement touched different parts of Burma including the southern Chin state, Kachin areas, Falam, Tiddim that could also stimulate the youth for the cause of the movement. The Zo leaders also approached the embassies of the USA, UK and India, and sought support from Bangladesh. The response of India was very restrictive and reserved for two reasons. India did not like to irk relationship with Burma and was apprehensive of the movement leaders getting involved in political activities. They however got moral support from the ethnic brethren in border areas of Manipur and Mizoram.

Zomi Re-unification Movement: The India Chapter

The Zo leaders, on the eve of Indian independence, decided to enter Indian Union on the condition that "the Lushai hills" will be allowed to opt out of the Indian Union, when they wished to after a period of ten years. Correspondingly in the same year, the Zos in Burma also signed the historic "Panglong Accord, 1947" in which they, the trans-frontier people such as the Shan and others, agreed to join the Union of Burma on the condition of secession from Burma whenever they wished. These two resolutions of the Zo leaders were historically significant. The Chin National Union in 1933 submitted a memorandum to the British Government in Rangoon demanding independence when Burma was given independence. Another organisation, called Chin Leaders Freedom League, was formed to free the Zo country from Japanese oppression that later merged with the Sukte Independence Army.

On the Indian side of the border, a representative of the Zos submitted a memorandum to Sir Robert Reid in 1940, urging him to take steps for territorial re-unification of all their inhabited areas in the spirit of the Chin-Lushai Conference (1892). Thus, the Zo unification movement in India from the very beginning had a cross-border ramification. The Zo leaders from Manipur and Burma agreed to fight for re-unification of the Zos across the border. In the Mizo hills, the Manipur Mizo Integration Council (MMIC) was leading similar movement for Mizo unification and greater Mizoram almost like Zogam encompassing the Mizo inhabited areas of North-East. In order to legitimise its stand, the MMIC extended support to the similar demand of the Nagas in Manipur, the Bengalis of Cachar, to Mikir Hills to join with Meghalaya and to the Maitheis for a full-fledged statehood or remain with the Mizo areas (Ray).

Patriotism apart from their common ethnic affiliation was an added factor that strengthened the unification movement. This gave birth to an ethno-nationalism that went across and beyond the territorial limits of the nation state. Ethno-nationalism of the Zo people also contested the methodological nationalism of the Burmese and Indian states. But the relationship of the Zomi leaders with the MNF was not comfortable although both were fighting for a similar cause. In the 1960s, both Mizo National Front (MNF) and Paite National Council (PNC) submitted memorandum to the Government of India demanding "unification and integration" of their people. The PNC made a demand for Chinland that could accommodate as many as 30 allied tribes encapsulated as "Chin". Besides the PNC, some other organisations came up with the demand for Chinland including the Chinland Independence Organisation (CIO), Chin Democratic Party (CDP), and CLA. Later, the CIO was changed to the Zomi National Front (ZNF). The UMFO, MNF, Mizo Congress Party, PC Party and ZNC also fought for re-unification. The ZNC of Manipur also organised a big convention at Champhai, Mizoram in 1988, mobilised the Zo people from all corners and resolved to work for re-unification.

In 1991, Zo re-unification was re-organised as a non-political organisation and went up to the United Nations with their demands. In the second Zo convention held at Aizawl on 17th July 1991, it was resolved to continue the movement on a non-political platform.

All these organisations were dreaming for trans-border integration. The ZNC, Manipur tried to mobilise their support for struggle for *"Zogam"* (land of the Zomis). However, the ZNC reduced its demand for Union territorial status in India. This marked a departure from its earlier stand. John Khawkimthang of CNF in his address to the UN Conference of Indigenous People in Geneva on 27th July 1994 declared in the spirit of the ZORO charter, "The Chin or Asho Chin, also known as the Kuki, called themselves Zo, Mizo, Asho, Zomi, Laimi, etc., formed as a nation before the advent of the British. However in 1890, our country was subdued and divided into three administrative segments and annexed to India, Burma and Bengal by the British Government for administrative convenience and it remained divided till today".

In 1995, the ZORO submitted memorandum to the UN Secretary-General for re-unification of the Zo people under one administrative head. The ZORO became greatest champion for re-unification drawing on the spirit of the Chin-Lushai Conference of 1892. The ZORO with its headquarters at Aizawl has access to the United Nations and participated in the United Nations Working group on Indigenous Peoples (UNWGIP) session held at the UN Headquarters Geneva in 1999.

The democratic movement of the Zo people in India underwent a fluid process of inter-ethnic alignment and re-alignment to suit the need of the time. Under the banner of the ZORO, the democratic movement was rejuvenated. The strategic alignment of Zomi Revolutionary Organisation (ZRO), a Manipur-based organisation, changed over time when the later aligned with the United Peoples' Front (UPF), an umbrella body of seven militant groups. The other constituent groups of the UPF are the Kuki National Front,

United Kuki Liberation Front, Kuki Revolutionary Army (Unification), Zou Defence Volunteers, Hmar People's Front (Democratic) and Zomi Revolutionary Front. The UPF has been pressing for a separate state out of the five hill districts within Manipur. The Zomi unification movement is standing on critical crossroads. The demand is creation of a state within a state under the provisions of Article 244 of the Constitution of India for fulfillment of the socio-economic, linguistic, cultural, infrastructural, educational and developmental aspirations of the hill people of Manipur.

References

Das JN (1987): *A Study of the Land System of Manipur* (Gauhati: The Law Research Institute of Eastern Region, Gauhati High Court).

Goswami, Sanjib (2010): "Legal Pluralism and the Administration of Justice in North-East India", paper presented in the *Conference on Non Adversarial Justice: Implications for the Legal System and Society,* organised by A I J A and Faculty of Law, Monash University, 4th May.

Hluna John, V (2011): *North-East Umbrella* (Shillong: DBCCI Sacred Heart Theo. College), 185-198.

Krawsthanga (2013): "Insuihkhawm"(in Mizo), *A Zofest 2012. Souvenir* (Aizawl: MZP).

Ray, Asok Kumar: "The Issue of Mizo Integration", *Journal of NEICSSR,* 12(2): 46-48.

Sanga, R (2012): "The Manipur (Village Authority in Hill Areas) Act, 1956, paper presented in the seminar on *Tribal Issues In Manipur,* organised by The Steering Committee on Mega Manipur Tribal Seminar at TRI Auditoroum, Imphal, 7-8 December.

(2013): *The Telegraph,* Guwahati, 18th March.

Vumson (1986): *Zo History* (Aizawl: Vumson).

Zathang, Piang (1982): "The Tribal Village Chief- Dead or Alive", in *Young Paite Association Annual Magazine,* Churachandpur, Manipur, II: 46.

ZRO (2013): Zomi Re-unification Organisation: Truth and Freedom, Re-unification Movement: After the British Rule: In Burma, available at *http://www.zogam.org/home/htm,* viewed on 12th June 2013.

SECTION–IV: PEACE EDUCATION

11

Promoting Democracy and Peace Education in North-East India

Leban Serto

Introduction

North-East (NE) India is a picturesque, having diverse cultural setting and many communities inhabiting the region. The contemporary reality of the NE, as in many parts of the country and the world, is one of deep violence. There are various armed ethnic outfits aspiring for their own ethno-nationalism. The combination of high technology and seemingly endless ethnic conflict has become the pattern of our times. Behind all of this is the expansion of a new ideology that legitimises a culture of violence, a culture of death, to suit a particular agenda for aggression. As a result, insecurity, fear and anxiety characterise the lives of many people. This culture of violence manifests itself in different ways. There is the negative impact of economic globalisation, which continues to widen the gap between the "haves" and "have-nots". There is also the structural violence of domineering or negligent governments in relation to the populations. Corruption and the abuse of power often manifest themselves in violence. In addition, there are often structural forms of violence, prevalent in the societies. These also result in gender discrimination based on community and class. Then, surrounding our very life is the violence against the environment. An important study on the anthropology of violence among the various ethnic groups could give importance to the endemic nature of violence in the region (Leach 2008).

Dilip Simeon (2002) commented, "Communal and caste violence has become the preferred mode of governance of the Indian ruling classes, the mode by which they have negotiated their discomforts with democracy. The periodic outbreaks of mass murders that we call 'riots' can no longer be explained away as unfortunate tangents in an otherwise steady course of India's development. They are the very face of Indian modernity. Unless we abolish the enemy system, we will transfer its burden to our children. And that will be a crime which will not wash easily".

It is in this context of growing violence that the need for peace education is growing. In the words of Betty Reardon (1988), peace education deals with the conceptual core of violence, its control, reduction and elimination. Presently, some forms of overt violence prevailing in the country are: (i) Naxalite and Maoist movements are presently growing and about 165 of the 602 districts in 22 states are affected; (ii) In NE India, there are various armed ethnic outfits aspiring for their own nationalism. Many tribes have their own armed outfits. Militarisation is also growing in the region, young people are being recruited in the government armies, at the same time, there is also recruitment among the ethnic armed groups; (iii) There is a growing militarisation of the government army in almost all the tribal belts in India; (iv) Unemployment among youths is growing in most of the conflict areas in the country; (v) Caste and communal politics is increasing the polarisation of the Indian communities; (*vi*) Gender discrimination and violence against ethnic minorities, tribals and *dalits* are increasing in institutions and major cities; (vii) There is increase in HIV/AIDS among young people, especially in the conflict areas; (viii) Religious fundamentalism is increasing. Education is being defined from the perspectives of the major communities and not necessarily on scientific lines in some aspects. Minor ethnic groups are forced to assimilate and learn the major languages.

Some Basic Facts: North-East India (2001 Census)

India's North-East, spreads over an area of 262,179 sq. km and consists of eight states (provinces) viz., Assam, Arunachal Pradesh, Manipur, Meghalaya, Mizoram, Nagaland, Tripura and Sikkim. It is stretched between 89.46 degree to 97.30 degree East longitude and 21.57 degree to 29.30 degree North latitude. The region has 4,500 km long international border with countries, namely, Bangladesh, Bhutan, Burma (Myanmar), China and Nepal. The whole region is connected with the rest of the country by a tenuous 22 km land corridor through Siliguri in the eastern state of West Bengal, a link that has come to be referred to as the "Chicken's Neck".

There are about 442 languages and dialects speaking groups of people with distinct cultural and ethnic identity. Comprising only eight per cent of the country's geographical area, the NE is home to a total of 39,035,582 people (2001 census), which is 3.80 per cent of the country's population. It includes 20,162,752 males and 18,872,830 females, with a density of 149 persons per sq. km., which is much less than the national population density of 324. The decadal growth of population of the NE states in absolute numbers is 7,081,811. There are 936 females per 1,000 males in the region, which is marginally better than the national ratio of 933. The total number of children in the region is 6,246,327.

Assam is the most highly populated state in the NE, with a population of 26,638,407 and Sikkim the least with 540,493 people. Sikkim has the highest incidence of poverty in the region. Mizoram has the highest literacy rate in the entire NE with a literacy rate of 88.49 and Arunachal Pradesh is the least literate state with 54.74. Incidentally, Mizoram is the second most literate state in the country. The state also ranks highest among the north-eastern states in the human resource development index.

The entire region can be geographically divided into two parts: plains and the hills. The majority of those living in the plains of the region are Hindus and Muslims, while a substantial proportion of the hill tribes inhabiting the states of Meghalaya, Mizoram, Manipur and Nagaland are Christians. The most populous part of the region is the Brahmaputra valley in Assam, which constitutes about 22 per cent of the region. There are stark differences among the eight north-eastern states with respect to their resource endowments, levels of industrialisation, as well as infrastructural facilities. The economy of all states remains underdeveloped and primarily agrarian with very weak industrial sectors and inflated service sectors. The industrial sector has mainly developed around tea, oil, timber in Assam and mining saw mills and plywood factories in other parts of the region.

The North-East India, wedged between Bhutan, Bangladesh, Myanmar and China's Tibet region, is a turbulent frontier. Insurgency and ethnic strife plague the region, retarding its progress and economic activity. A cursory look at the socio-political dynamics of the NE reveals lack of livelihood opportunities, despite immense natural resources of the region. This bred insurgency, and insurgency, in turn, has hindered the growth. The cycle, if anything, is vicious.

The region is inhabited by hundreds of different communities and groups having distinct languages, cultures, religions and history. With the exception of Assam, Tripura, and Manipur, where non-tribal populations are dominant, the rest of the region is populated mostly by tribes. For instance, in Tripura, the predominantly tribal population, which was over 53 per cent during the early part of the 20th century, has shrunk to 31 per cent in 1991. Under the Constitution of India, the tribes are categorised as the "Scheduled Tribes". The region has seen a large influx of immigration (environmental refugees, economic migrants) from Bangladesh, which is rapidly changing the demographic landscape of the region. The territorial/border dispute with China along the borders of Arunachal Pradesh, which had already escalated into the 1962 Indo-China war, has put the region under the high security radar.

Conflict Issues in the North-East: Socio-political Situation

The political turmoil and armed struggle is found all along the region. It began with the Nagas struggle for political self-determination, which dates back to the 1940s. The Mizo National Front (MNF) followed this in the 1960s. In Assam, what started as a movement to protect the Assamese identity against the immigrants from Bangladesh during the 1970s turned to self-determination under the United Liberation Front of Assam (ULFA). Nonetheless, the issue around the "illegal immigrants" from Bangladesh is a major political discourse in the region. The clash between the Bengali settlers, who came during the colonial period to Assam with the majority of Assamese people over resources and linguistic identity, is one good example. Another conflict in Assam is the Bodo tribal group seeking a separate federal state. It was partially settled when the Bodoland Autonomous Council was granted. There are several tribal groups in Assam like the Karbis, the Kachari, and the Dimasa who are seeking special status in the political set-up.

In 1964, the United National Liberation Front was formed in Manipur, demanding a separate state. In 1978, a more radical organisation, called the People's Liberation Army, emerged. In Tripura, various organisations were formed by the 1960s demanding tribal autonomy who found themselves "internally colonised" within their homeland. Meghalaya has also seen the emergence of various social organisations demanding tribal protection against encroachment from "outsiders". Arunachal Pradesh, the only state in the region that has enjoyed "negative peace", has in recent times experienced the overflow of violence of the various militant groups, particularly from Assam and Nagaland. Today there are more than five militant groups operating in the state.

It is estimated that there are more than fifty militant groups in the North-East region. Political interests and demands directed towards the Government of India vary between the various tribes and ethnic groups in the NE. But it is becoming clear that the people of the region have to monitor and explore their political demands and interests in relation to each other by opening up to the possibility of negotiation and accommodation in terms of territorial, boundaries, resources and trade while meditating with the Government of India. The policy of competition and lack of dialogue between the NE states, either through the directives of Delhi or power interests, has cost thousands of lives.

Issue of AFSPA

In the region, the Indian army operates under the Armed Forces (Special Powers) Act 1958. This Act permits even non-commissioned officers "to fire upon or otherwise use force, even to the causing of death, against any person who is acting in contravention of any law or order..." The Act also guarantees complete immunity. It reads, "no prosecution, suit or other legal proceeding shall lie in any court of law against any officer of the armed forces in respect of anything...".

Governance

The NE is characterised by the absence of good governance and lack of a political will by the Government of India to develop a system to accommodate the needs of the indigenous communities. The imposition of its unitary will by the Indian state has become one of the major challenges for the unity and vibrancy of the Indian Union and its democracy. The Government of India policy of military oppression, appeasement and economic incentives (in this order) has not addressed or solved the various problems in the region, which are political in character. Rather it has produced alienation, violence, insurgency, instability, lack of trust and accountability in the governmental machinery and policy.

Corruption, extortion and criminality have become rampant in the region. Poverty is becoming widespread. The cleavages of inequality in an otherwise tribal ethos of egalitarianism are becoming wider. The people of this region are "intimidated by gun-toting elements and silenced either by fear or confusion or despondency" by the various militant groups, the corruption and the threat of the governmental bureaucracy and the aggressive behaviour of the military troops. The legitimate ongoing struggle for survival, identity and recognition of the people of the region is by no means redundant because of the means and behaviour of their own militant groups. One journalist pointed out the political and social situation in the region as a culture that "promotes a dreadful silence". In the current culture of "dreadful silence", the masses are "mute", not because they are "dumb or deaf", but because they are made silent by the various power blocks and collusion. The culture has prohibited the people to engage creatively and participate in the transformation and reconstruction of their society.

Highlights of Some Crucial Issues Confronting the Country

India is home to more than one billion people. The national goals are derived from a magnificent history, strong interaction with Western societies and great heroes like Aurobindo, Tagore, Gandhi, Nehru and others. Baptist missionaries also pioneered and contributed towards the development of education. Seerampore in West Bengal was the hotbed for a mini Danish cultural revolution in the 18th century. It was a safe haven for missionaries, and in 1799, Baptist missionaries set-up Asia's first printing press here. In 1819, William Carey established the Seerampore College, the first of its kind, to impart Western education in Asia and translated the Bible into local dialects (Subramaniam 2012).

Most government actions are now directed from the top of national and state bureaucracies and most individuals and communities have little voice. Many government programmes are not effective because those served, often poor and illiterate, have no power to deal with their public servants. There is a continuing problem of funding services at optimum levels. The mixture of limited services and the undue authority of officials create an imbalance of power with corruption and bribery often the norm in dealing with official agencies. In general, the educational systems are based on an old British model combined with large number of students from poorly educated families. Major competitions for jobs and government stipends stifle individual creativity and contributions. There is a long prevalent history of bribes, payoffs and kickbacks at every level of the government. Many in the government feel they have the right to get as much as they can, since they have been downtrodden and exploited.

Unless a new attitude emerges, the people will continue to distrust their government and continue to be exploited. A new thinking, a new attitude, must emerge in individuals in order to become informed, honest and fully participating citizens. These attitudes can be taught and applied to life throughout the school years. This large educational system needs major modification that will require large number of people to change their attitude and behaviour. We believe, teaching peace education, social justice and bringing global education to the doorstep will equip the present generations to understand the various issues facing the mankind today.

National Council for Educational Research and Training (NCERT)

The formation of the National Focus Group can indeed be viewed as a progressive step taken by the Central government. Out of the 21 focus groups, peace education has also found a way under the chairmanship of Valson Thampu. In India, the National Curriculum Framework (NCF) 2005 has recognised importance of peace education in the schools. A holistic perspective helps learners to observe both the direct and indirect relationships between forms and violence at all levels as well as the values, practices, and necessary conditions needed to overcome them.

Situation in Schools and Higher Education in the Country

The Indian school system is the most complex and multi-layered in the world, marked by diversities, inequalities and inadequacies of various minds. For education for peace to have a realistic chance to deliver within this system, it is important that the likely pitfalls and potholes along the route of implementation be remedially engaged. From a pragmatic standpoint, the preference for the integrative approach is dictated by anxieties about curriculum load. But, surely this cannot be a greater priority than enabling education to engage its goals, nor should it be assumed that peace is a "burden" or the only burden, from which students are to be protected. In fact, peace is a blessing rather than a burden. The NCF 2005 wishes to make an impassioned plea that education for peace should not be strategised and implemented from an outlook of anxiety about "curriculum burden", lest this pioneering initiative be foredoomed. Peace if it is to work at all has to be prioritised. Nothing less will do.

Education and Issue of National Integration

One of the emotional issues raised by the NCF 2005 is of national integration. The education system is seeking ways and means to integrate the country through promoting the culture of peace stating that the life of a nation is, at all times, in a state of continual evolution. Cultural agents are key players in this process. They share or disfigure the India of our dreams. Of late, the conflict of cultural paradigms has assumed special intensity. A triangular pattern may be noticed in the ongoing confrontation of cultures: cultural homogeneity, cultural plurality and cultural subalternism. It states that the people of India in its Constitution have expressed themselves, in the language of democracy, against homogenisation as altogether alien to the spirit of India. Religious, linguistic and cultural plurality is innate in its history and heritage. With these goals, integration has become the ideal pedagogy for peace education in India. The pedagogic strategy for education for peace presupposes in this is that of integration. Integration is the ideal since peace is an integrative and all embracing concept. But this ideal approach is to be implemented in a system that is far from ideal.

The ground realities concerning every constituent of education—from textbook writing to classroom teaching, from teacher motivation to the school setting—leaves much to be desired. Education for peace reckons the reality of the alarming increase in violence in school life. The NCF also deals with reference to the two major goals of education, namely, education for personality formation and education to foster responsible citizenship. Citizenship, not religion, is what all Indians share in common.

There is a plea made to turn education for peace into a people's movement. A few notes of caution are also given. The enterprise of education must be cleansed of social and gender injustice; for what is tainted with injustice cannot be a vehicle of peace. Letting the minds of children—the citizens of tomorrow—be warped by violence is a serious problem and it needs to be acknowledged and addressed with the seriousness and urgency it merits. Peace must be pursued with single-minded vigour and an undeviating sense of purpose. Education for peace as a pioneering movement must be implemented with vision and determination. A casual or half-hearted attempt could trivialise it and aggravates cynicism about its efficacy (NCF 2005).

The Asian Highways and the North-East

The increasing emerging role of the Association of South East Asia Nations (ASEAN) has coined a slogan "one community one destiny" and Look East Policy (LEP) remarked by Hillary Clinton on its strategic importance and the 2013 budget allocation has given a fillip to India's LEP. Besides giving a leg-up to the economic prosperity of the north-eastern states, the LEP holds immense strategic importance for the country. The LEP begins with Myanmar, which is taking a baby-step towards democracy and coming out of international isolation. This will immensely impact the NE.

Asian Highway (AH) project, also known as the Great Asian Highway, is a cooperative project among the countries in Asia and Europe and the United Nations, Economic and Social Commission for Asia and the Pacific (ESCAP) to improve the highway systems in Asia. It is one of the three pillars of Asian Land Transport Infrastructure Development (ALTID) project, endorsed by the ESCAP commission at its forty-eighth session in 1992, comprising Asian Highway, Trans-Asian Railway (TAR) and facilitation of land transport projects. In recent years, agreements have been signed by 32 countries to allow the highway to cross the continent and also reach Europe. Some of the countries taking part in the highway are India, Sri Lanka, Pakistan, China, Japan, South Korea and Bangladesh. A significant part of the funding comes from the larger or advanced nations as well as international agencies such as the Asian Development Bank (ADB). AH1 is the longest route of the Asian Highway Network, running 12,845 miles (20,557 km) from Tokyo, Japan via Korea, China, Southeast Asia, India, Pakistan, Afghanistan and Iran to the border between Turkey and connecting with Europe via Bulgaria (AH5). In India, the AH1 is 11,432 km (7,145 miles).

The brief description of the Asian Highway projects should develop an immense interest and challenge, especially to the people of the NE. Though the works have commenced and discussion and consultation have started, there are skeptics who think the project is too ambitious and is next to impossible. On the other hand, the civil and political strife across nations in some Asian countries is also hindering the progress and work of the Asian Highways. North and South Korean stalemate, the fragile situation in Myanmar and insurgency issue in NE India, the war like situation in Pakistan and war in Afghanistan are causing immense concern. It is a reality that the Asian Highway will pass through these conflict areas and regions in near future. The need for preparing the people is crucial. Therefore, the challenge before us is that, it becomes an important rallying point to develop strategies how we could prepare the communities in NE India.

India's Situation and Response to the Asian Highways

India's LEP was implemented for the first time in 1992 when India became a sectoral dialogue partner with ASEAN. The LEP is believed to enable India to create good bilateral relations with the South East Asian countries, which assist in the development of country's trade, commerce, and transportation. Recently in 2006, the government approved to go ahead with construction of the Integrated Check Post (ICP) at its international borders. There are four ICPs to be built in the first phase—Attari-Wagah, Raxual, Petrapole and Moreh—out of the 13 proposed. It is important that the civil societies, government and community leaders work together to formulate long-term plans for the phenomenal changes and try to benefit from the coming of the Asian Highways in the NE. The Government of Inda along with ASEAN is conducting a series of car rallies to bring awareness in the region (Goswami 2009; Serto 2011).

Emerging Issues of Nationalism

Nation-building is a dynamic process. It refers to the process of constructing or structuring a national identity using the power of the state. This process aims at the unification of the people within the state, so that it remains politically stable and viable in the long run. Nation-building can involve the use of propaganda or major infrastructure development to foster social harmony and economic growth. Today in NE India, the issue is being articulated by communities based on their common origins, culture, and language. Plague with political aspirations, almost all the ethnic groups have their own frontal armed groups. The region has also witness deep violence. It is necessary to address the importance and need for democracy and peace education. Carloyn Stephenson (2005) stated, "Nation-building is a normative concept that means different things to different people. The latest conceptualisation is essentially that nation-building programmes are those in which dysfunctional or unstable or 'failed states' or economies are given assistance in the development of governmental infrastructure, civil society, dispute resolution mechanisms, as well as economic assistance, in order to increase stability. Nation-building generally assumes that someone or something is doing the building intentionally".

Working towards a Solution–Need for Spiritual Awakening and Good Governance

In a rapidly changing socio-political and economic landscape, a critical exploration of what does being tribal, belonging to their respective federal units in the NE in relation to the Indian Union mean to them is essential. Any major political or economic development in NE India cannot be discussed in isolation within the region only. The Government of India plays a huge role. The asymmetric power relationship of Government of India and NE India cannot be discounted. Major structural change cannot come unless the policy of legitimised power domination evolves into a more relational interdependent policy. Such a shift, however, would need collective pressure from NE India, a sensitised bureaucratic system and a political will from Government of India. Development, reconciliation, unity (multi-cultural unity as opposed to unipolar unity) and peace cannot be achieved without challenging the "dreadful silence". The challenge is to make the people become more conscious of their plight, their rights and prepare them to speak collectively by giving them a platform. It is necessary to empower the people and give them support to have a sense of collectiveness without necessarily denouncing their particularities and common interests so that the culture of "dreadful silence" can be defied and people can reclaim the right to their voice.

A two-pronged strategy of conflict resolution and prevention of conflict can be both applied when we think of the region as a whole. But the importance of the various ethnicities must be given importance. Each tribe is important and, at the same time, how to bridge across the differences with the overall objective of promoting democracy and national objectives at large is also important. The children are exposed to so much of violence, be it on the TV, in newspapers or in real life. It is becoming importantly crucial that this be addressed within the context of the educational system. So that in the long run, students have the idea of creating a better world which is tolerance. In order to explore and find some possibilities organising workshops, targetting teachers, community leaders and members of various NGOs, who will be the main instruments in bringing these desired objectives, are necessary. Social analysis of the situation and developing local capacities for peace are important (Brendt 2006).

The challenge for individual or organisation, who wants to bring constructive changes, is to examine the ground realities and reach the majority of people in the region who are politically powerless, economically poor, culturally discriminated and socially outcaste. It is to locate the majority subalterns within the subaltern NE region. It is also to develop an alternative politics of interpretation through accommodation, negotiation, consultation, respect, education and advocacy. Such a politics has to emerge from the "conscientised victims of the dominant structures of nation-building as a cultural, economic and political project". The possibility of such an interpretation could allow to develop a political system/institution that would give the people a sense of security, ownership and accountability. Such a task, such a calling, is a continuous process that constantly challenges the social status quo by becoming more aware of our spirituality, integrity and compassion that we are capable of as well as the biases and prejudices we can all exhibit if not addressed within the self. The challenge, however, is very exciting because in the NE, the human capital of the community is vibrant and very strong. If this enormous resource can be tapped, empowered, managed and allowed to take on more responsibility for their immediate social reality and relationship than a just and a more fair society is almost feasible. Despite the evolving politics of power and domination in NE India, the sense of tribal egalitarianism, of justice and equality in essence remains. This, we believe, is still alive and will lead each and every member to fight against poverty, and freedom from fear of domination and suppression (North East Region Vision 2020).

Need for Peace Education

Peace education is about learning skills to relate non-violently. The Tirana Call (2005) stated, "Peace education is a participatory holistic process that includes teaching for and about democracy and human rights, non-violence, social and economic justice, gender equality, environmental sustainability, disarmament, traditional peace practices and human security". It included representatives of ministries of education, inter-governmental and civil society organisations convened by the Hague Appeal for Peace on 20-23 October 2004 in Tirana, Albania. The methodology of peace education encourages reflection, critical thinking, cooperation, and responsible action. It promotes multi-culturalism and is based on values of dignity, equality and respect. Peace education is intended to prepare students for democratic participation in schools and society.

Peace education is a diverse and continually changing field, responding to developments in society and, to some extent, to the advancing knowledge and insights of peace research. As practised in elementary and secondary schools and presented in the university programmes that prepare classroom teachers, peace education goes by various names: conflict resolution, multi-cultural education, development education, world order studies, and more recently, environmental education. Each of these approaches responds to a particular set of problems that have been perceived as the causes of social injustice, conflict and war (Reardon 1988; Hague Appeal for Peace 1999).

One of the important things to bear in mind is that peace education performs two important functions in a curriculum. First, it unites all other subjects under the holistic vision of peace. In the absence of such a holistic view, the learning done in subject compartments tends to be fragmentary and remain superficial. Secondly, peace education humanises education. It is a humanistic approach to education rather than a subject. Any lesson in any subject could be presented through the peace approach with full justice without formal knowledge of the use of peace education approach in their lessons and classroom management. This shows that such an approach is integral in good education. However, theoretical and practical knowledge can improve their present classroom practices. The present situation beckons us to work for peace (Jeyaseelan 2008).

The task of peace education is the dissemination of peace knowledge primarily through preparation for action. It facilitates learning to intervene in situations of lack of peace, learning how to take action as responsible citizens. Also learning the skills and knowledge required for effective action. Good peace education helps students learn to make arguments based on sound analysis and contextualised interpretation. It helps them determine the types of policies and intervention that follows from those arguments and hopefully opens to them the possibilities to take action. Such goals, of course, have always characterised progressive educations' approach to education for citizenships and democracy (Harris 1999).

Peace Education Activities in North-East India

In the state of Manipur during September 2000, with the formation of the Centre for Peace Education Manipur (CFPEM), a series of awareness workshops, campaign and teachers training was conducted. Apart from these, networking with other organisations in different parts of the NE was worked out. Highlighting and promoting Global Campaign for Peace Education (GCPE), numerous campaigns were held advocating the need for peace education at the institutional and communities levels. More so, among people groups affected/afflicted by violent armed conflicts in the region.

One of the earliest groups attracted to the ideas is the faith-based organisations like the Baptists and Catholic institutions. An initial pilot project, "Orientation of Teachers to Teach for Peace" was held in the year 2005-2006. The project reached out to the government and private institutions supported by the Catholic Relief Services (CRS). A power point presentation with the title "Peace is" which highlights the speech of Aung San Suu Kyi that was smuggled out and presented at the Hague Appeal for Peace was translated and widely circulated. In April 2007, a regional workshop on the theme, "Peace Education for All in North-East India" was held in Shillong. The workshop was funded by the North-East Council (NEC), Government of India. In December 2007, another workshop on "Peace Education for All in India" was organised at the Gandhi Bhavan, Delhi University, in collaboration with NGOs and institutions like Miranda House and St. Stephen College. The workshop was model along the lines of Community-based Institute on Peace Education (CIPE), the first CIPE in India held in 2007. The second CIPE in India was held in Orissa in 2009.

Incorporating Peace Counts on Tours (PCoT) and Travelling with Gandhi Project

The Department of Peace Studies in the Martin Luther Christian University (MLCU), Shillong incorporated peace education as one of its course paper. During 6-8 November 2010, the department convened the consortium titled "Embracing Peace Education – Empowering the Individual, Institutions and Communities" with special focus on India. Training of Trainers (ToT) by Peace Counts on Tour was held in March 2009, New Delhi. This author began to incorporate the ideas of peace education and stories of the PCoT in workshop and teachings in order to enhance peace education campaign and movement in the NE. A series of exhibitions of PCoT is also conducted in the region. In March 2010, this author initiated a project, "Travelling with Gandhi", with the aim to instill the ideals and ethos of Gandhi's principle of non-violence to the youths of the NE. Efforts have been made to influence communities, state governments and universities in the region to incorporate the need for peace education for conflict transformation and building a culture of peace in the region. But still much remains to be done.

North-East India: Peace Education Literatures

Some of the literary works on peace education in the NE are *Peace Education* by Leiren Singh (2003); *A Quest for Peace in the North-East,* compiled edition by L. Jeyaseelan (2003); *The Search for Peace in North-East* by Charles Chasie (2005). 'Importance of Peace Education in Universities' by this author (2007) is a paper presented at a seminar at MLCU, organised by Indian Council of Social Science Research (ICSSR), Shillong. *Teaching for Peace and Peace Curriculum in Manipur,* by this author (2011), is a research finding on the need for peace education in Manipur. Jayaseelan (2004) is of the opinion that a long drawn conflict contributes negatively to the growth of the state on many fronts. The absence of peace has weakened relationships, societal ties between ethnic communities all in the name of man-made differences. Pupils should be made to realise that conflict and confrontation have not taken any community, society, nation to progress and development. Conflict played out in the open field without any rule and regulation is self-destructive. The curriculum has to enable our youth to produce the positive energy of peace, which can be reintroduced through peace education. Adopting alternative ways to solving conflicts learning skills such as dialogue, mediation and negotiations, sitting across the table, become partners in dialogue and move on the path of reconciliation.

Strategies for Peace Building in the North-East: Some Suggested Steps

The following suggestions are developed from years of working in the field of peace studies and peace education promotion.

Political Will and Reforms

There is a need for political will to reform the education system to make it suitable for promoting peace ideals and peace educational projects. To have high quality research conducted in the emerging field of peace education by the University Grants Commission (UGC), Indian Council of Social Science Research (ICSSR), reputed defence studies and theological institutions in collaboration with NGOs, individuals and noted Gandhian institutions. Constitute a body of eminent citizens to oversee and make reports to facilitate peace programme in the NE.

Knowledge and Conceptual Clarity

To promote orientation and outreach at the teachers training institute, refreshers courses in colleges and encourage workshops and seminars at various levels: school, higher secondary to the level of universities. To develop clear concept and theory of peace and peace education. To familiarise with the practices and emerging trends of peace education. To promote teachers training institute with the state-of-the-art. To urgently evaluate the contents of the educational curriculum and see if they are leading to some violence. To inculcate peace values among students and youth. Also to orient theological leaders, community leaders, and political class/political parties at varies level.

Research and Publications

To increase the libraries on peace education. To encourage publications of journals on peace education, via internet, e-groups, book publications, etc. To make different strategies for states and regions. To provide sound understanding of the subject and not a half and ad hoc approach to peace education. Educational institutions must be encouraged to come out with good quality publications on a regular interval. The NGOs working in the field of peace and development must also be encouraged to share their project reports and best practices. Regular manuals and teaching kits must be prepared and developed.

Plans and Implementation

It is important that educational department/institutions have comprehensive plan and components of human rights and peace education in the teachers training programme. Also in children's curriculum. To create a plan of National Peace Index along the lines of the Global Peace Index (GPI 2011) with national objective and parameters. The states must also encourage creating a state peace index. There must be studies for interventions, violent prevention, human right education, national goals. To create a healthy link between the schools, government boards and universities on regular intervals. To involve them in joint projects towards better delivery, enhancement of skills, performance and governance.

To make education more humane, it needs to infuse components of Gandhian ideals and sustainable development goals. To involve community leaders and educationists in creating educational reforms at various levels. Components of human rights, dignity, and tolerance of cultural and religious diversity be taught from primary level. To involve faith-based organisations, NGOs, civil societies, traditional educational system in building peace education. To create centre and mobile training centres to impart training and update skills and performance. To urgently incorporate the Millennium Development Goals 2015 (MDG 2010) along with the peace programmes at hand. To make Gandhian ideals more attractive to young children and encourage collaboration with schools and universities and faith-based organisations.

Paulo Friere's Teaching in Relation to the North-East India Situation

Education can be an agent of social transformation in the region. It can enable the people to shun violence and adapt non-violent revolutionary means to achieve their goal. Freire's participatory education and problematisation to conscientisation are all means to a revolutionary end. Such a pedagogical process of Freire's should challenge the people to be committed to the revolutionary process. Freire's methodology for adult education or learning is relevant in the context of the North-East, especially in social learning situations. Friere's thought on liberative education such as popular participation, dialogue, problematisation, critical consciousness or conscientisation and revolutionary praxis could provide enlightenment and motivation, and enhance people's involvement for social transformation in the region (Friere 1972; Sema 2011).

Monitoring and Evaluation (M&E)

To monitor and evaluate the performance of the educational sectors if they are in tune with the needs of the communities and the country at large. To evaluate the performance of the bureaucracy in the delivery system of the national education policy. To develop tools for M&E for enhancing the quality and standard of the education and peace programme. To create robust intervention, where there are lacunae and need urgent intervention along the lines of International Network of Emergency Education (INEE). To evaluate and access the quality of teachers at the state/national training centres. To monitor whether standard and sufficient training is being imparted to enhance their performance. To be updated with the need of times. To encourage collaboration with centre of excellence in the state, regional centre and global level.

Peace education must find a prominent place in the schools and universities all over NE India. The coming generation should not be deprived of learning such a crucial knowledge, research and skills, which could enhance their adaptability to survive on this planet (Connel and Curle 1985). The knowledge, skills and most important, the values that have been at the core of peace education for the past five decades are those required to meet the new peace challenges and opportunities of the 21st century (Cebezudo and Reardon 2002).

The issue of national integration is important as much as tolerance and inclusiveness of all communities within the country must be given a fair deal. Education must not be divisive or segregated. The acknowledgment of education in India as a fundamental right for all children in the age groups of six to 14 is a potential revolution, if its implication is addressed earnestly. This call for a reform and participation for education to be converted into a people's movement and communities are empowered to participate in the process. An approach to education that erodes social cohesion, aggravate economic inequalities and undermines ethical foundations needs to be recognised as a threat to peace and a disservice to society (NCF 2005).

Conclusion

In order to face the challenge of our times, we need to explore all the avenues through which we could combat the growth of intolerance, violence, arm race, environmental exploitation, racism, etc. Learning for communal harmony and non-jingoistic ways is important. Education must help develop skills of tolerance and communal harmony. Training of teachers to teach for peace is crucial step for intervention in conflict regions. Prevention of inter-group violence and deadly conflict with emphasis on "super ordinate goals" (Humburg 1999) must form an important component for the design of conflict study and peace education for the NE. There is an urgent need to introduce peace education into our schools and universities as this will humanise the present education system and help the young minds prepare for peace in the coming century.

In any nation-building process, there is a danger of segregation and exclusion. A relook at the nation-building process requires that democracy and peace education must be incorporated in our education and political system in order to create vibrant communities and people in NE India in the 21st century.

References

2008: *North Eastern Region Vision 2020,* Ministry of the Development of the North Eastern Region Council, 13th May.

Brendt, Hagen (2006): "People Building Peace – Transforming Violent Conflict in South Asia" (Bonn Germany: Evangelishcher Entwicklungsdienst), September, 88-89.

Charles, Chasie (2005): *The Search for Peace in North-East,* Peace Studies paper-03 (Guwahati: Omeo Kumar Das Institute of Social Change and Development).

Connel, O and A Curle (1985): "The Scope of Dilemma of Peace Studies" in J 'O Connel and Curle (ed.), *Peace with Work to Do: The Academic* (Learnington Spa. Warwickshire Berg, Publisher), 29-5.

Dilip, Simeon (2002): "The Enemy System", *The Hindustan Times,* New Delhi, 6 December.

Education for Peace (2006): *National Curriculum Framework, 2005,* Position paper National Focus Group (New Delhi: NCERT).

Embracing Peace Education (2010): Consortium, Shillong, available at Newsletter # 78 /www.peace-ed-campaign.org/newsletter/archives/78.html viewed on 10th January 2012.

Freire, Paulo (1972): *Pedagogy of the Oppressed* (Penguin Books Ltd.).

Goswami, Namrata (2009): *Looking East through India's Identifying Policy Challenges and Outlining the Responses,* Occasional paper no. 2 (New Delhi: Institute for Defence Studies and Analysis).

Hague Appeal for Peace. (1999): available at *www.haguepeace.org,* viewed on 2nd September 2010.

Harris, Ian (1999): "Peace Education", in *Colleges and Universities in World Encyclopaedias of Violence, Peace and Conflict* (San Diego CA: Elsevier Science and Technologies Books), 12: 679-689.

Humburg, David A (1999): *Preventing Contemporary Intergroup Violence and Education for Conflict Resolution* (Carnegie Corporation of New York: Carnegie Commission on Preventing Deadly Conflict).

Kieman, Ben (2008): "The Pol Pot Regime"- Race, Power, and Genocide in Cambodia under the Khmer Rouge, 1975-79.

Leach, James (2008): "Talk Given in the Course Introduction to Anthropology", at 1501 lecture 19, at the University of Aberdeen.

Leiren, L Singh (2003): "Peace Education: Reflections" (Imphal: Philosophy Department, Manipur University), May, I(I).

LEP (2010): available at *http://www.rediff.com/news/report/look-east-policy-brings-india-into-asia-pacific-clinton/20130201.html,* viewed on 5th January 2012.

Lokendro, Arambam (2005): *Peace Process in Manipur. Armed Conflict, State Repression and Women,* Peace Studies Paper-2 (Guwahati: Omeo Kumar Das Institute of Social Change and Development).

Macintyre, Tim and Camilla Schippa (2011): *Global Peace Index, GPI* (Institute for Economic and Peace).

Nani, Gopal Mahanta (2005): *Assam: Portent of Violence and Hope for Peace,* Peace Studies Paper-3 (Guwahati: Omeo Kumar Das Institute of Social Change and Development).

National Curriculum Framework (2005): *Position Paper National Focus Group on Education for Peace (3.4), 2006* (New Delhi: National Council of Educational Research and Training), September.

OKD Institute for Social Change (2008): "Pre-emptive Peace Education - Is Peace Education Necessary in the Present Context", seminar organised by OKD Institute for Social Change during 26-27 February.

Peace Counts on Tour (2012): available at *http://www.aja-online.org/en/peace-counts/about-peace-counts/* viewed on 4th May 2012.

Peace Education for all in India (2007): available at *http://www.i-i-p-e.org/cipe/indiareport.pdf,* viewed on 25th February 2012.

Reardon and Cabezubo A (2002): *Rational for the Approach to Peace Education and Learning to Abolish War,* Hague Appeal for Peace, Books I, II and III, available at *www.haguepeace.org,* viewed on 26th June 2012,

Sema, Akheto (2011): *Understanding the Nature and Purpose of Christian Religious Education,* (Delhi ISPCK – Indian Society for Promoting Christian Knowledge), revised ed.

Serto, Leban (2007): "Importance of Peace Education in Universities", a paper presented at Martin Luther Christian University, Shillong during the *MLCU Consultative Workshop on Peace Education* on 6th March, organised by ICSSR-NERC, Shillong.

Serto, Leban (2011): "Promoting Peace Education along the Asian Highway (AH) No.1", Paper presented at the *New Agenda for Peace Research in the Asia-Pacific* on 14th-16th October, organised by Asia Pacific Peace Research Associate (APPRA), the Graduate School of International Relations and the Kyoto Museum for World Peace, Ritsumeikan University, Kyoto, Japan.

The MDG Report (2010): "Millenium Development Goal Report, 2010", New York.

Tirana Call, Peace and Disarmament Education (2005): "Lesson from Four Countries, Albania, Niger, Peru and Cambodia", UN Department of Disarmament Affairs (UNDDA) and the Hague Appeal for Peace, available at *www.haguepeace.org,106,* viewed on 23rd March 2010.

SECTION–V: BEYOND THE HORIZON

12

Colonialism vs Chieftainship

(The Making of Colonial "Agent" in Chin Hills)

Pum Khan Pau

This paper presents the Zo encounter with the British and the consequent establishment of colonial administration in Chin Hills, now Chin state in western Myanmar, in the late 19th century. It is divided into three parts. The first part introduces pre-colonial Zo political systems in Haka, Tedim and Falam areas, respectively. While the second part seeks to discuss British perception of Zo chieftainship and how they dealt with it, the establishment of the "indirect rule"[1] by the enactment of the Chin Hills Regulation which redefined the power and functions of the chiefs and turned them into "agents" of colonial project is examined in the third part.

Zo Political System: Haka, Tedim and Falam

Traditional political systems of the Zo in Chin Hills may be studied based on three hill tracts—Haka, Tedim and Falam.

Haka Tract

Prominent clans found in the Haka tract include Lai, Laizo, Thantlang, Zokhua, Thetta, Lautu, Zathang, Zophei, etc. The Haka polity is best represented in F.K. Lehman's (1980: 139-140) monumental work, *The Structure of Chin Society*. The Hakas had *"khua bawi"* (village headmen) who governed the village together with a *"tlangpi"* (council) and one or more subsidiary officers, in particular the *"tlangbawi"*, or village ritual officer. The office of the headman is usually hereditary. While some have autocratic powers, some lean more heavily upon their councilors (Lehman 1980: 139-140). Haka had not a single paramount chief of its own. However, there were powerful clans like the Zathangs whose several local branches each had a chief, each such chief having a realm of satellites and allies.

Tedim Tract

The Sukte (also the Kamhau), Guite, Sizang, Thado, Zou, etc., were the major clans in the Tedim tract. The *"hausa"* is the headman of the village. He owned the land and collected taxes such as paddy tax, salt tax, meat tax, bee tax, etc., and other dues from the people within his jurisdiction. The institution of *"hausa"* was usually hereditary. The *"hausa"* was assisted by members of the village council called *"upa"*. Besides, the *"siksek"* (blacksmith), *"tangko"* (village crier), *"tulpi/ siampi"* (village priest) were also closely associated with the *"hausa"*.

There were more powerful *"hausa"* of a village who exerted influence on weaker ones and collected taxes[2] from them and created a realm of dominance. Such *"hausa"* referred to themselves as *"mang"*, a noble term given to distinguish them from a mere village *"hausa"*. They were actually what Lehman (op.cit: 26) called the "supralocal chieftaincies". The status of a *"mang"* mainly stems from "tribute relations"[3] where the vanquished would give tax or tribute to the conqueror for a stipulated period, if not permanently. Thus, by the end of the 18th century, a number of clan-based *"mangs"* such as *"Sukte mang"*, *"Guite mang"*, *"Thawmte mang"*, etc., already emerged from the status of a mere clan chief or village headman. They were occasionally fighting with each other for greater political dominance and economic interests.

One who was superior to the *"hausa"* and *"mang"* was the *"ukpi"*, a paramount ruler/chief.[4] One of the most powerful

Sukte ukpi was Khan Thuam of Mualbem.[5] He levied all forms of customary dues and tributes from villages under his control, which stretched from territories of present-day Manipur in the north to Falam tract in the south. According to the tradition, during this period the *"Poi-gal"* as it was often referred to for the Falam invasion was so feared in the north that villages not legally recognised by the *"Sukte ukpi"* were liable to be invaded by the Falams. Here is a song composed by Khan Thuam, which succinctly described the extent of his dominance.

> *Siahtaang kaihna sak ciang Teimei/Ka hialna Lamtui hi e.*
> *Sak ciang Teimei sang ciang Lamtui/a lai ah kamkei hi'ng e.*
>
> [Translation]:
>
> What I rule extends to Manipur in the north/and ends at Falam in the south.
>
> Manipur to the north and Falam to the south/I am the tiger in the middle (Khai 1995: 26).

In 1848 Kam Hau, the eldest son of Khan Thuam, who established himself as a powerful chief at Tedim, curved out his realm of dominance from the Sukte tract. Kam Hau's sway extended to more than 130 villages that the people under his control became known after his name. It was during the rule of Khaw Cin, the *"Sukte ukpi"* that the British attacked Tedim.

Falam Tract

In the Falam tract was found the Taisun, Shunkla, Khuangli, Ngawn, Khualsim, Thawr, Zahau, etc. Unlike the Haka and Tedim tracts, a democratic political system was found in Falam tract. Henry Noel Cochrane Stevenson, a Burma frontier service officer who was stationed at Falam for quite some time, remarked that prior to the annexation, the Zanniat and the Tashon were democratic tribes whose villages were ruled by councils of elders called *"Nam kap"* selected to represent village quarters or in some cases patrilineal extended families. These he labelled the democratic group.

As regards to the emergence of a democratic council in Falam, this is what Carey and Tuck (1983: 142) had to say,

> "Four generations ago the ancestors of the Shunklas of Falam migrated from Shunkla and founded Klashun, and, at the same time, another family also quitted the nest and fitted to Saiyo. They had hardly got comfortably settled down before the Haka chief Lien Norn, the great-grandfather of the present chief Lyen Mo, attacked and destroyed both villages and scattered the inhabitants, who for years lived in settlements as fugitives. However, in course of time, the Shunklas made their peace with the Hakas and returned to found new village, which is the present Falam. After the Shunklas had founded Falam, they gradually brought all their neighbours, both relations and aliens, under their control. When we occupied Chinland we found the Tashons numerically the most powerful tribe in the hills, though we believe that had our occupation been deferred for two or three years the Yahows would have broken from their bondage, and Rumklao and Minkin would have declared for Haka, in which case the Tashon would have suffered in prestige as well as in possessions".

The Falam tribe was administered by a council of five chiefs, who were all chosen from the Shunkla tribe and from Falam village. The post of councilor was attained, not by virtue of birth, but by the vote of the people (*Ibid*: 149).

Source of the Chief's Power

According to Carey and Tuck, the chiefs were "lords of the soil" within their boundaries, and if any aliens wish to enter a chief's territory and work his land, they must pay him customary tithes. Besides the tithes, a chief also received tribute from tribes, villages or families which he had conquered (*Ibid*: 201). He also received one hind leg of every animal sacrificed by any of his men for religious purposes as religious tax called *"sa-khua"*. In some cases, the chief also served as village priest. There were two kinds of priest—the village priest known as *"tual-siampupa"*, *"khua-sampa"* or *"tual-phuisam"* in Tedim and *"tlangbawi"* in Lai, and the clan or family priest called *"tulpipa"* in Tedim (Khai 1995: 162-163).

According to Lian Sakhong (2003: 36), the chief "in traditional Chin society received the mandate of religious power and political authority from the '*khua-hrum*'. Because of this mandate, he and his descendents had the privilege and the right to control the entire land within the sovereign of *'khua-hrum'*, which was believed to be the guardian of the land". Therefore, Zo concept of political power is not a human invention but the mandate of the *"khuasiam/khua-hrum/khua-rung"* (in Zotung).

Political power, religious belief and the economic system were intertwined in chieftainship because, actually, it was not the chief but the god or spirit, which became the guardian of the land or place of settlement. The people observe the social codes not because the gods or spirits to whom sacrifices were offered demand, but because they feared the retributive punishment which was bound to ensue if one was indiscreet enough to ignore it. Sing Khaw Khai (1995:147) rightly says, "Zo society is the one in which there was no secular authority to enforce social justice nor was there any god or king, who gave the moral laws and administered them...It is a society where people believe in the existence of an unseen power that enforces social justice".

It may further be said that in early days there was no definite village territory or tract. The area of a new settlement was ritually defined. The founding of new settlement meant to them the setting up of the communal altar and the site where it was set-up is termed *"tual"* in Tedim. Thus, the ritually defined area is under the influence of *"tual"*. By ritual act, the *"tual"* territory was defined and *"tual"* state was created.

To get a clearer picture, it must be mentioned that Zo tradition classified mankind into two, namely, *"khual"* and *"tual"* in Tedim and *"khual"* and *"lai"* in Haka. *"Khual"* refers to non-member of the society, including foreigners and enemy, whereas *"tual"* implies the same member of the society or citizen of the village. *"Khual"* is further classified into two, viz., *"khuasat tuikhuat pawl"*, descendants of the founders of the settlement or aborigines/indigenous, and *"peemta"* refers to sojourners and captives from raids. *"Tual"* and *"khual"* did not eat and drink together. If one did so, the *"khual"* or enemy/foreigner with whom he ate and drank together must be reckoned as the same member of the tribe and could no longer be killed or avenged upon as duty-bound like enemy. An enemy became *"tual"* in the event that he had already drunk the water of wooden trough or *"kongkuang-tui"* (*Ibid:* 142-43).

Later on, village territory was defined on the basis of natural boundaries. Vumson (1986: 8) says, "A village was an independent unit, claiming land about seven miles or eleven kilometers in radius for its cultivation".

Though there were some variations in Zo political systems in the three tracts discussed above, there is one thing common to all. Whether it was autocratic or democratic political system, the chief(s) derived its power from the *"tual"* state. It would be interesting to see how the British sought to deal with the politico-religious and economically intertwined Zo political system in the late 19th century.

From Contact to Conquest: Colonial Perception and their Dealing with the Chiefs

Zo people had come into contact with the British in Arakan and Manipur even before the annexation of upper Burma following the Third Anglo-Burmese War (1885-1886). The annexation, however, was the beginning of a more important problem of pacification for the British, which took them at least another five years. Resistance in the form of guerrilla warfare started in upper Burma and spread to lower Burma too. "When the larger units of the regular army were broken up", wrote J.S. Furnivall, "scattered bands under local chieftains all over the country carried on guerrilla warfare". It was from this frontier that the British were to penetrate into the Chin Hills. Therefore, the British policy towards the Zo may be seen in the larger context of the political formulations in upper Burma in particular and Burma in general.

Traditional Burmese system of local administration was based on the circle under a hereditary circle headman, exercising a personal authority over his own people but not necessarily the overlord of all the inhabitants of the circle. When Charles Crosthwaite was appointed as the Chief Commission of Burma in 1887, he saw the political condition ripe for a change in the Burmese system. Accordingly, he "introduced a new system of breaking up the circles into villages, and a village act passed as an instrument of martial law, imposed on both headmen and villagers' duties under penal sanction without conferring on them any rights" (Furnivall 1948: 74). The village system thus substituted the circle system.

Crosthwaite, having soon realised that the Kabaw-Kale valley was quite exposed to raids from the hills, laid out his plan for dealing with the Zo. He said, "The only system of government was that of headmen of villages, or at the most of a small group of villages, and consequently negotiations with the Chins as a people were impossible" (Crosthwaite 1912: 287). Perhaps, Crosthwaite may not have been fully informed about the differing political systems of Chin Hills. Nevertheless, certain events which occurred in 1887 were enough to caution the chief commissioner from any misadventure into the Chin Hills. Reports of eleven hundred thousand Taisun surrounding Indin, three hundred marching to Taungdwin, three hundred on Kalewa; five hundred Sizang raiding Kalemyo and another six hundred threatening the Kabaw valley. Although these numbers might possibly be a bit exaggerated, they nevertheless influenced upon

Crosthwaite's decision not to resort to immediate military expedition.

Therefore, negotiations ensued. In March 1887, F.D. Raikes, Deputy Commissioner of the Upper Chindwin District, met representatives of the Taisun in Indin and told them to stop raiding. On 26th December, Raikes held a meeting with the Sizang chiefs at Kalemyo followed by another durbar with the Falam Chief Con Bik at Sihaung in the Kale valley (*Ibid:* 288-289; Carey and Tuck 1983: 22-23). Negotiations continued with other Zo chiefs on different occasions.

It was the failure to bring Zo chiefs to their terms, which ultimately left the chief commissioner to opt for military expeditions in 1888. The scheme of operations sketched out by the chief commissioner and later approved by the supreme government was a clear reflection of British perception of the Zo chiefs. The military column was divided into two—the Northern column and the Southern column. While the former was entrusted with the Tedim area with its base at Fort White, the latter would based at Kan in the Myittha valley and to move into the Haka and Zokhua areas. The two columns were to make simultaneous attack on Falam (Crosthwaite: 310).

How the British regarded Zo chief as a sovereign power, if not their equal, may be reflected from a few official reports and diaries. David Ross, Assistant Commissioner with Southern column of Chin-Lushai Expeditionary Force, in his diary on 10th January 1890 wrote, "After satisfying ourselves that these men were the duly authorised representatives of the Yokwa people and that promises made by them would be observed by the whole of the people in the Yokwa circle, we proceeded to explain our terms to them..." (NAI 1890: 147). Similar statement was made by W.P. Symons, commanding the Chin-Lushai Expeditionary Force on 1st May 1890, "That we would make no treaty, nor discuss terms with any but chiefs" was the first and foremost terms given to the Chins. Symons further added, "Much delay and difficulty was experienced in dealing with the Chins on account of the numbers of chiefs with each tribe. There is no central controlling authority. Each chief has a following, and all are bitterly jealous one of the other. Negotiations, therefore, had to be carried on with extreme patience" (NIA 1891: 171).

To add more, during the 1888-89 operations, Carey reported, "the Siyin tribe had lost every village in their country and the Kanhaws no less than 17 villages, and yet this wholesale burning and destruction was followed by no satisfactory results; not a single chief had surrendered" (NAI 1891: 126). On another occasion, he said, "only chiefs and members of chief's families be arrested are/and that the ordinary inhabitants would be of no use to me, whilst a few chiefs and chiefs' relations in our hands would be a powerful incentive to induce the villages ruled by these chiefs to surrender" (NIA 1890: 256). Carey did not entertain even the headman as he said, "The Sagyilain headman came in and wished to speak to me. I refused to see him, sending back word that until the chief came in, I would not have any conversation with the village" (*Ibid*: 7).

Redefined Political System: "Indirect Rule" in Chin Hills

It took at least three years for the British to subdue Zo chiefs who steadfastly offered stiff resistance, though actual colonial administration was in place only in 1896. The long series of surveys and expeditions had thrown up a good deal of information on the chiefs, the clans and the villages. It was clear from these that in any future system of management of the Chin Hills, the chiefs would have to be an integral part.

The report on the administration of the Chin Hills for the year 1895-96 was fully of optimism which declared, "Peace and order have been maintained throughout the district." In January 1896, a draft regulation was ready for the future management of the Chin Hills. This was based on the south Lushai Hills model of the Bengal Government and, more particularly, the system that had been followed in the Kachin Hills. Indeed, the proposed draft regulation was based on the Kachin Hills Regulation (I of 1895) enacted a year earlier.

The regulation was to apply only to tracts which were from time to time brought under administration. In the Chief Secretary's letter forwarding the draft regulation it was made clear that "the regulation aims at the least possible interference with local customs and preserves the autonomy of tribes and villages. At the same time, full and sufficient powers are reserved to the Superintendent for the purpose of control and supervision". The powers and functions of the Superintendent and the duties and obligations of the chiefs or headmen were accordingly defined. The Superintendent was to be Deputy Commissioner, District Magistrate, and Sessions Judge, his assistants, sub-divisional officers and assistant collectors would be invested under the code of criminal procedure with necessary magisterial powers.

What was crucial for the Chin Hills, however, was the superintendent's relations with and control over the chiefs, or headmen as the regulation termed them. The term was so defined as, "headman" means the chief or head of any clan or village inhabited by the Chins, and includes a council of chiefs or elders. A clan was any sub-division or section of Zo and included a group of Zo; a village included, "a village community", "village lands", "rivers passing through or by village lands" and a "group of villages".

Chapter III was devoted to headman and their powers. Section 5(1) of the draft thus stated: Subject to any general or special orders of the local government, the Superintendent may appoint and remove any headman, and may define the local limits of his jurisdiction and declare what clan, or village, or both shall be subject to him. Sub-section (2) added, "Where a headman is appointed for a group of villages or clans, the Superintendent may declare the extent to, and the manner in which the headman of the villages or clans composing such groups shall be subordinate to the headman of the group".

The headman was given, within the local limits of his jurisdiction, general control according to local custom, over the clan, or village or both, declared subject to him. He could levy from them any customary duties and impose such punishments as authorised by local custom. Other sections bound him to keep the peace within his jurisdiction, to comply with all lawful orders of the Superintendent or his assistants, to furnish them on requisition and on receipt of payment at rates fixed by the Superintendent, supplies of food or labour required by any public servant. The headman was given the authority of criminal jurisdiction, and could punish with fine in money or goods any person found guilty by him of any offence within such jurisdiction. As regards civil jurisdiction, he could try and decide according to local custom any dispute of a civil nature between persons subjects to his general control and could enforce his decision. The last Chapter VII, prohibited appeals : "There shall be no appeal against any order passed by a headman or by an officer acting under this regulation".

Although the headmen were to act according to custom and usage, the powers granted to them by the regulation were far greater than that which they traditionally enjoyed. But the overall control and supervision by the Superintendent permeated every section of the draft regulation. Section 38(1) for instance proposed, "All headmen and all officers in the Chin Hills shall be subordinate to the Superintendent, who may revise any order passed by any such headman or officer, including an assistant superintendent...".

No new village could be formed without the consent of the Superintendent, "who may, for reason to be recorded in writing, prohibit the formation thereof". In addition, he had powers to direct the removal of villages.

The regulation thus followed the pattern of "indirect rule" on the model of the South Lushai and Kachin Hills. The essential difference between the Lushai Hills and Chin Hills situation lay in the fact that in the former there was only the village chief. Here, the policy, described by Chittagong Commissioner David Reid Lyall, was "recognising a chief from each village and not recognising any one chief as paramount over any tract or country". In the Northern Chin hills, the position of Hau Cin Khup had to be recognised and strengthened, while at Falam the importance of the council had to be taken into consideration.

The draft regulation was considered in the legislative department of the Government of India, which after amendments was approved by the Governor-General in Council on 23rd July 1896. It was Gazetted on 15th August (Gazette of India 1896).

Conclusion

The policy that Carey and his officers were working out for the Chin Hills was, thus, not unique, but part of a system that came to be well-known as "indirect rule" or administration.[6] According to Michael H. Fisher, "Indirect rule is the exercise of determinative and exclusive political control by one corporate body over a nominally sovereign state, a control recognised by both sides". He further adds, "One of the most fundamental problems in indirect rule is the issue of sovereignty of the local ruler...Indirect rule demands that the theory of sovereignty be modified from its usual absolute form" (1991: 6 and 13). For an effective and cheap administration in the Chin Hills, the British continued the indigenous mode of village administration through the chief, who in fact was redesignated as headman, respecting and preserving tribal laws and customs. Thus, they retained the existing chiefs and appointed new ones. The chiefs were reduced to a subordinate position and were required to recognise the British supremacy.

Interestingly, the source of the chief's power stemmed no longer from the "tual" state but from the colonial state to enforce its project. The chief or headman, therefore, became the "original political agent" as Timothy Earl (2011: 30-31) rightly says. And the British officers became overlords to the Zo chiefs. The regulation established feudal form of colonial administration, which was to last for another half a century. Following the departure of the British from Burma, colonial sponsored chieftainship also came to an end in 1948, which may be considered as the beginning of democratisation process of Zo indigenous political system; a remarkable day being celebrated by the Zo as Zo Minam Ni on 20th February, thenceforth.

Notes

1. Based on Michael H Fisher (1991): *Indirect Rule in India: Residents and the Residency System 1764-1857.*
2. Taxes collected by such chiefs mainly comprised: *Mim siah/tang siah, sial lampi sap, tuikuang tui siah, in saliang, gam saliang, tuk tha khal tha, inn zangsial lamsa, tuk an khal an.*
3. For further discussion, see Abraham I. Pershits (1979): "Tribute Relations", in *Political Anthropology.*
4. How the *ukpi* emerged is an interesting story. The earliest *Sukte mang* was Kaih Mang of Mualbem. In the late eighteenth century Khan Thuam, the son of Mang Kim, emerged as a potential contender to the reigning *Sukte mang.* His rise also posed serious threat to the position of other *mangs* of Tedim region. Khan Thuam's initial success, therefore, provoked a combination of *mang-kua* (nine *mangs* of different clans) against him, and he was soon obliged to flee to Falam country and took shelter under the protection of Rallang chief Khuang Ceu by giving tribute to him. With the help of Khuang Ceu Khan Thuam and his eldest son Kam Hau were able to overcome all opposition. After his position became relatively secure, he returned to Mualbem, the capital of the Sukte clan, where he assumed all the trappings of a chief. After he consolidated his position at Mualbem he avenged all those who had conspired upon his life, and also embarked upon territorial expansion in the now well-known Tedim and Tonzang regions, pushing in the process several tribes towards the northern fringes.
5. Administrative titles of rulers of the northern hill tract may be mainly categorised into three: *hausa* or *tulpi* is a clan chief or village chief or priest; *mang* refers to supra-local chief or chief who exerted influence over more than one village by dint of his power to collect taxes; *ukpi/ukpipa/innpipa* is one who is paramount and whose sway extends to a large tract comprising numerous village chiefs and tributary-tribes. He is an autocratic ruler who enjoys formidable

power and control over a large tract. Each village headman or chief within his jurisdiction owed allegiance to him and paid all perquisite dues. The term *per se* is believed to be equivalent to the Indian title Raja.

6. See Note in FEAP, October 1896, Nos. 28-35.

7. For an account of this, refer Michael H Fisher, *Indirect Rule...*; D.A. Low (1973): *Lion Rampant,* London. For its operation in the Khasi and Jaintia Hills, D.R. Syiemlieh (1986): *British Administration in Meghalaya: Policy and Pattern* (New Delhi), p. 69ff. For the situation in Africa where it became famous in Nigeria, see Margery Perham (1962): *Native Administration in Nigeria* (London).

References

Carey, Bertram S and HN Tuck (1983): *The Chin Hills* (New Delhi: Cultural Publishing House), 1, first published 1896.

Crosthwaite, Charles (1912): *The Pacification of Burma* (London).

Earle, Timothy (2011): "Chief, Chieftaincies, Chiefdoms, and Chiefly Confederacies: Power in the Evolution of Political Systems", *Social Evolution and History,* 10(1): 30-31.

Fisher, Michael H (1991): *Indirect Rule in India: Residents and the Residency System 1764-1857* (Delhi: OUP).

Furnivall, JS (1948): *Colonial Policy and Practice: A comparative study of Burma and Netherlands India* (Cambridge: Cambridge University Press).

Gazette of India, Regulation No. V, 15th August 1896 (also published in the *Burma Gazette).*

Guite, Chinkholian (1999): *Politico-Economic Development of the Tribals of Manipur: A study of the Zomis* (New Delhi: Anmol Publications).

Khai, Sing Khaw (1995): *Zo People and their Culture* (Churachandpur: Khampu Hatzaw).

Lehman, FK (1980): *The Structure of Chin Society* (USA: University of Illinois, reprint by Aizawl: Tribal Research Institute), first published 1963.

National Archive of India, FEA, April 1890.

National Archive of India, FEA, March 1891.

National Archive of India, New Delhi, Foreign Department, External-A, March 1890.

Pershits, Abraham I (1979): "Tribute Relations", in S Lee Seaton and HJM Claessen (ed.), *Political Anthropology* (The Hague: Mouton Publishers).

Sakhong, Lian (2003): *In Search of Chin Identity* (Copenhagen: NIAS Press).

Seaton, S Lee and HJM Claessen eds. (1979): *Political Anthropology* (The Hague Mouton Publishers).

Syiemlieh, DR (1986): *British Administration in Meghalaya: Policy and Pattern* (New Delhi).

Vumson (1986): *Zo History* (Aizawl: Vumson).

13

Development Perspective vis-à-vis Ethnic Aspirations with Special Emphasis to Manipur

Valte Vungzamuan

This paper is akin to a comparison between Mahatma Gandhi and B.R. Ambedkar as the emancipator of *Dalits* in India. For the majority of Indians, Gandhiji was the *Messiah* of *Dalits*; but a *Dalit* identifies himself with Ambedkar for empowerment.

The British Policy

The colonial administration concerning the hill tribes in general was to keep them secluded with the policy of least interference in their way of life. The policy was to uphold the government of the chief, to govern through them, rather than to try to govern without them. The basic objectives of the Chin Hill Regulation 1896, the East Bengal Frontier Regulation 1873, the Excluded and Partially Excluded Areas Order 1936, etc., were to keep the tribes in check and keep them away from interfering and harming the interests of the British subjects, a protective shield for the British settlements, to achieve their own economic interests. It was not the primary objective of these provisions to safeguard the tribesmen from the plain's people, which however turned to be a provision for safeguarding the interests of the minority tribal communities from being submerged, subsumed, exploited and assimilated by the majority communities around them. In fact, it created buffer zones in certain pockets such as Chin Hills, Lushai Hills, Khasi Hills, Naga Hills, etc., and help in containing the depredations of the tribesmen against British subjects. In fact, the concept of sepoy villages was even introduced in Manipur, arming the Kukis as a protective shield against the raids by Kamhau/Sailo clans into Manipur valley.

Policy of Independent India

The tribesmen were allowed to continue their own systems of governance through chieftainship where the village/clan chief plays an important role in the day-to-day life of his subjects. The British administration adopted the easier route of governing these areas through the clan/village chiefs, either in administration of justice or in collection of levies and taxes. This system of village administration was continued by the Independent India, allowing the tribes to govern themselves in their own traditional ways, such as customary practices and beliefs. The continuations of the Inner Line Permit system, Sixth Schedule provisions, Foreigners Restricted Area Order 1963, etc., by Independent India were testimony to this policy. However, some constitutional experts strongly feel that India's minority policy might someday prove to be a Pandora's box, the white man's burden, incitement of separatism, breeds exclusivity and goes against the spirit of the federal structure of the Constitution of India.

Political Awakening of the Tribes

The 1940's witnessed social and cultural movements primarily fuelled by the desire to have their own say in the political affairs of their future, in the eventual of the departure of the British from India and Burma. The political turmoil and its aftermath led to the birth of several movements for homeland and ingrained in them the son of the soil theory. Many tribes rejected the old system of self-governance through lordship of the chieftains, and especially in the Chin Hill the democratic movement culminated in the abolition of chief's rights in 1948. Such was the intensity that it led to the birth of the Naga National Council, the Mizo Union, the Kuki National Assembly, the Khulmi National Union, the Hmar National Union (HNU), etc., coming into being one after another with far-reaching ramifications for the tribes, as well as the region in general. In the aftermath of this political turmoil, certain tribal pockets were made into tribal autonomous councils such as Khasi, Jaintia and Garo Hills, Lushai Hills and the state of Nagaland was declared in 1962 (effective from 1963) with certain safeguards, under a special dispensation.

Valley and Hill Divide in Manipur

In the state of Manipur since independence, several attempts were made to bridge the divide between the hills and the valley which were traditionally separate from each other in terms of religion, customs and practices, ethnicity, etc. In fact, after the subjugation of the tribes after the Kuki Rebellion in 1919, the tribes were brought within the ambit of the British administration but governance was through the village chiefs. Immediately after independence in 1947, the Manipur State Constitution Act, 1947 was enacted and a provisional council was constituted and elections were held in 1948. Along with the enactment of the Constitution Act of 1947, an enactment was also made in the form and style of the Manipur Hill Peoples (administration) Regulation, 1947. This enactment specifically empowered the village chiefs as chairman to administer justice and maintain law and order. However, the merger of Manipur with the Union of India on 15 October 1949, thereby recognising the state of Manipur as a part "C" state of the Union of India had brought the earlier enactment to naught.

Nationalist Movements amongst the Tribes

The wild fire of nationalist movement in Nagaland and Lushai Hills (Mizoram) caught the imagination of the marginalised tribes who were sandwiched between the Manipur valley and Mizoram, on the one hand, and between

Nagaland and Manipur valley, on the other. Attempts at unification of the Naga tribes were met with some measure of success and most of the tribes joined the movement for a Nagalim (greater Nagaland), even though a parallel Zaliangrong movement went on for quite some time. In the meantime, the Kuki movement for independence, consolidation and political settlement went on hand in hand with the Khulmi Union in Manipur. The Kuki movement and Khulmi movement succeeded by the Chin movement came in direct clash with the Mizo Union with serious consequences, especially amongst the Paite and the Hmar tribes. The Hmars clashed with the Kukis and the Paites migrated from Mizoram.

The successful abolition of chieftainship in Mizoram (1954) caught the imagination of the enlightened educated Christian lots, which led to clashes between the traditionalists and the reformists with much discomfort in certain pockets, especially in south Manipur. The Hmar tribes embraced the Mizo Union movement with the expectation of creating an autonomous district for all the Hmar settlements. The creation of Lushai Hills District Council in 1952 betrayed the hopes of the Hmar community, thereby leading to the formation of the HNU.

Local Self-government in Manipur

Till 1956, the hill areas remained largely un-administrated with little participation of the local people in any democratic process, except on occasions of election to the Manipur Legislative Assembly. In 1956, the Manipur Village Authorities (in hill areas) Act, 1956 was enacted by an Act of Parliament, thereby introducing, for the first time, a local body of self-governance at the local level (village). It introduces a system of election to the village body which will be headed by the chief (ex-officio chairman). However, the power of the chief has been curtailed to some extent in the formation of village courts to be manned by two members of the elected members, to be appointed by the government.

This enactment does not address the issues of participation in planning and execution of developmental works; it merely empowers the village courts to administer justice within the limited powers given to them under the Schedule to the Act (offences punishable with a fine only upto two hundred rupees) etc.. Eventually, the Government of Manipur issued a notification in 1971 entrusting/empowering the village authorities to identify and select beneficiaries under poverty alleviation schemes, review all development works within the village, formulate and supervise village development schemes, help government agencies, receive grant in aids, donations and receive subsidies. It also envisages the setting up of village development committee (VDC) to assist the village authorities in carrying out their assigned functions. It is indeed a salutary step towards democratisation of the hill administration in Manipur.

District Councils in Manipur

The Government of India placed the hill districts of Manipur under the Fifth Schedule (on the basis of the A.V. Thakkar sub-committee report) by an Act of Parliament. The Manipur (Hill Areas) District Councils Act, 1971 as amended, read with The Manipur Legislative Assembly Hill Areas Committee Order 1972 under Article 173-C of the Constitution of India, came into force. On the other hand, in the valley local level administration under the Panchayati Raj system (the Panchayati Raj Acts of 1975, 1994 and 1996) at the grassroots level and urban bodies in larger towns have been implemented with measurable successes.

The objectives of the district councils were, to address the developmental needs of the tribes, protection of their land, preservation of their customary laws and practices and democratisation of the administration. Unlike the district councils under the provisions of the Sixth Schedule, these district councils were neither autonomous nor democratic in the sense that no provision for regional council was made available. There was no provision for linkages with the local bodies and no block level elected bodies was created. It is a stand-alone council, providing glorified debating platforms without any real authority/autonomy.

Drawback of the Scheme

In spite of several attempts at enhancing the powers of the councils, it was doomed for failure from the very start in as much as no financial autonomy was given. It depends upon grants given by the state government. It also has no legislative power (cannot make laws) and no judicial power (cannot set up council courts). The council administration functions under the direct supervision of the district administration, such as approving the budgetary proposals, legislative proposals, framing of rules and regulations, by-laws, development works, etc. The council members were mere followers of the ruling dispensation in the state and mostly do not possess original ideas and principles in political and policy matters. Their survival mostly depends on the satisfaction and goodwill of the ruling party in power.

Grassroots Democracy in the Hills

Democratisation of the hill administration under the provisions of the Sixth Schedule has been the bone of contention between the tribes and the Meitei valley dwellers for the past 40 years. The denial of justice for self-administration under the Sixth Schedule provision led to innumerable protests, strikes, boycott of elections, etc., for more than two decades with limited success. However, by an amendment in 2008, certain powers were added to the functions of the councils and elections were forced upon the tribes in 2010.

Attempts at democratisation of the village administration at the grassroots, proposal for amendment of the Manipur (Village Authorities in Hill Areas) Act in 2011 was also resisted upon by certain tribes, which however was the need of the hour in order to bring true democracy to the hill people. It proposes to do away with the position of ex-officio chairman enjoyed by the chiefs, to be replaced by a democratically elected institution and replacement of the term village authority to village council and expand the numbers of members. It also introduced election of chairman of the village council by members of the council. This is expected to bring about true democracy at the lowest level. However, the village courts, its functions, administrative set-up, salary for court officials, sitting allowances, etc., should be prescribed. At the district level, judges should be appointed to hear appeals arising out of decisions by the village courts, an enabling provision must be created for the enforcement of the customary laws and practices of the tribes (when codified).

The Scourge of Insurgency

The romanticism associated with freedom movements, homeland movements and movements for self-rule, autonomy, independence, etc., has its roots on the tribal milieu of the region. Tribalism in the form of inter-and intra-tribal rivalries was the product of a sense of insecurity amongst the tribes, the fear of being sub-merged, the fear of losing dominance, the fear of losing their land and the fear of losing their rights and privileges. One of the root causes is the prevalence of chieftainship system in the village administration amongst some of the hill tribes. Royalty and privileges enjoyed by such chiefs is hard to give up, leading to desperate attempts at maintenance of status quo at all costs. Groups espousing sovereignty sprouted all over, including the Meiteis trying to put the clock back, harping on the restoration of the old order, pre-historic times. The reasons for such movements may be diverse, in some cases restorative, in other cases reformative and in some cases preservation of the age-old traditions and practices.

From early times, the tribes in Manipur were split into two major blocks, the Naga group and the Kuki group. Again splinter groups emerging from everywhere—Khulmi National Union as a political party, then followed by the Hmars for a separate homeland, the Zomis for a separate administrative set-up plus re-unification, the Kukis for Kuki land, the Nagas for greater Nagaland and so on and so forth. It is a never ending process, each trying to upstage the other in the game of one-upmanship, either for political or territorial dominance. These groups staged protest of all sorts, including enforcement of bandhs and blockades, running for months together in their own areas of dominance leaving the general public high and dry. The culture of the gun which enveloped the entire political spectrum has had debilitating effects on the social milieu and economic life of the tribes in general.

The consequences of militancy, untold humanitarian sufferings inflicted, the opportunity costs and the economic costs, multiplying by the day cannot be measured by any means. Manipur's culture of violence and the power of the gun being endemic, it is a vicious circle with no end in sight and no easy solution to that. It is sad that in Manipur after every two kilometers or so, nothing is predictable, every step has to be watched carefully; else one may end up a victim of un-intended target of insurgents operating in small pockets. It is sad that human voices are stifled, economic life goes downhill, no industrial activity survives and above all no developmental activities can progress without splurging money to fill the coffers of insatiable marauding hordes of gun-totting criminals, extortionists, all in the name of freedom movement. It is said that no one dare to set-up a shop, built a house, buy a car, take up government contracts, etc., without the knowledge (permission) of the watchful and prying eyes of the numerous extra-constitutional functionaries, namely, the pseudo national freedom fighters.

Elections and its Implications

Electoral politics means big business, in such an exercise, clannish obligations/loyalties and tribal affinities came to the fore, totally blinded about the political ideologies of the political parties they represented. Elections are won on the platter with money power and gun power (support by myriad militant organisations). Distribution of party tickets, selection of candidates and selection of ministers at the time of ministry formation are all dictated by the tribal affinities (sans talent). Development programmes, planning, allocation of resources are all dictated by groups representing one section or another with the ulterior motives of filling their coffers popularly known as distributive justice.

A few examples will suffice to bring home the stark truth in this method of madness. The link language issue for a FM radio channel at Churachandpur took more than ten years to resolve, the problem for location of an FCI warehouse in Churachandpur was without any parallel elsewhere. The objection (read obstruction) to any development project, for instance the Tipaimukh dam project, is the result of such rivalries, be it pressure groups from the valley acting on militant dictates. Now, the unthinkable part, employments/ jobs are sold on ethnic lines with clannish tentacles spreading far and wide with no consideration whatsoever of merit.

Suggested Solutions

J.B. Fuller wrote in 1909, "...that the province of Assam at the far northeastern corner of India is a museum of nationalities". Experts believe that places inhabited by diverse ethnic minorities are excellent breeding grounds for conflicts, strife, warfare, civil disturbances, etc., because of the intense completion for meagre resources on ethnic lines. Nothing more can be true in the context of Manipur where the valley dwellers compete with the numerous tribes co-habiting the hills and also the tribes competing with each other for a pie of the land and its resources. Worst of all, gun-totting thugs rule the roost with little or no care for the well-being of the communities they represented. Extortion is rampant with no boundaries to demarcate their activities, which sometimes led to flare ups, conflicts and attempts at ethnic cleansing (at times).

The way forward to my mind, would be:

- Chieftainship breeds inequality, exploitation and stifled individual freedom (to utilise the land for productive use). Investment and credit system is hard to come by in such uncertain situation. Feudal set-up and land lordship of the chiefs should be re-examined and land ownership should be given to the community. Land survey, land reforms and introduction of land ceiling laws in the hills will bring about some level of accountability and transparency in land ownership patterns, and curb the autocratic powers of the chiefs with a view to prevent land related conflicts between the "haves" and the "have-nots". Wholesale sale of entire villages by chiefs must be prevented and abrogated. Minimum numbers of families to constitute a village must be prescribed and groupings carried out where necessary for ease of administration.

- As rightly noted by DONER at its website, "The hill areas of Manipur have been excluded from the purview of Part IX but without any provision for an alternative, creating vacuum in the legal frame for that area. It is of utmost importance and urgency that the hill districts are brought within the ambit of Sixth Schedule in tandem with other tribal dominated areas of the region".
- The romanticism associated with homeland movements of all sorts must be given a decent burial as it breeds conflicts, clannish loyalties, disunity and social discord. It hampers human and socio-economic developments, creating fear psychosis, public disturbances and, above all, undesirable civil wars. Such misadventures resulted in the loss of lives and properties (the wounds inflicted takes generations to heal), the ugly face of tribalism, an attempt to put the clock back. It is divisive, bred hostility, resulted in disintegration, with nothing to gain (the notion of a bye-gone era).
- In the discussion between Phizo and Morarji Desai, Phizo retorted to Desai, "How could Nagaland become a state of India?" Desai replied by saying, "It was the Nagas who came and asked for a state and it was given to them". The hollowness of Phizo's stand gets

exposed. The logic of being racially distinct, being culturally separate, being special, being different, etc., often espoused by cultural revolutionaries with an attempt to restore the old order (sovereignty) is all empty, hollow and deviant and is especially relevant to the Meiteis of Manipur. The activities of such revolutionary groups brought about a deep sense of insecurity amongst the tribes, forcing them to devise their own ideals of sovereignty/autonomy to safeguard their own interests. The recent movement towards de-sanskritisation of the majority community in the form of OBC status, demand for ILP and schedule tribe status is an area of major concern for the tribes. It is certainly a movement backwards but with far-reaching socio-political and economic implications for the tribes.

- The dreams and ideals for homeland, sovereignty, independence, autonomy, state within a state, etc., have been projected as remedies for all ills afflicting the society. Such romantic idealism thrives on sycophancy and deceit. It is an easy option to climb the social ladder, to become a master, amassing wealth for themselves like parasites, eating into the veins of the society like cancer. For them, the viability of a territory for self-administration is of no concern. This tendency led to divisive forces mushrooming all over in clannish fashions. It is a culture that needs to be forbidden for the common good. Bringing about reformation at the grassroots level, proper utilisation of the available resources, bringing about functional autonomy to the district councils and learning to utilise the powers/ authority made available, with a good measure of accountability and transparency must be engrained amongst the tribes. Else, there is no light at the end of the tunnel. The culture of dependence, as rightly pointed out by a Naga gentleman to me, "I feel very strongly that we need to build the economic pillar of Naga society, it is not healthy either for New Delhi or the Nagas to have a relationship that we have at the moment: a relationship of dependence..." is very aptly applicable for the entire North-East region, especially for the tribes living in Manipur.

- It is high time the natives look within themselves, put their heads together, bring about local self-administration (democracy) at the village level and stop lambasting the State government and Central government for all their self-inflicted wounds. Should they bring about revolutionary steps to usher new land reforms, new land tenure system and proper land records and establish urban bodies to cater to the ever-growing needs of their growing economy? Should they go for communisation of public institutions and services as is being done in Nagaland since 2002? That is, creating effective service delivery system in the villages run by elected representatives.

  Should they look at the North Eastern Region Vision 2020 for the codification of land records, land reforms, distribution and computerisation of land records, maximising self-governance, strengthen self-governing institutions, ensure maximum people's participation in the decision-making process at the grassroots level, etc., for their own sake? The answers lie with them. Because as Biren Singh, a minister in Manipur, said, "The Manipur Assembly passed the Manipur (Hill Areas) Act, 2008 only after the Hill Areas Com nittee (HAC) consented to it following a six-month study of the provisions. If the tribal population of Manipur did not like the Bill, no tribal Member of Legislative Assembly (MLA) would have had the courage to clear it in the HAC. The clearance by the HAC shows that the Act has the support of the tribal people (tribal MLAs) of Manipur". Truly, the tribes had played key roles and can certainly be the instruments of the much desired changes. Tribes should prove their ability to govern themselves in administrative capacity building and local practices. The elites should rise to the occasion and play a pivotal role in stemming the divisive tendencies engulfing the region.

- Religion plays a pivotal role in the socio-political and economic life of the tribes who professes to be hundred per cent Christians. Religious beliefs must be translated into good citizenry conduct such as loyalty to one's service, respect for the rule of law, respect for human life, exemplary conduct, accountability, transparency, etc. The present system of militant-politico nexus and the rampant corruption at all levels prevailing in the social fabrics of the tribes does not augur well for the future, betraying their own professed religious consciousness. The spirit of "*phatuamngaihna/ tlawmngaihna*" (camaraderie/altruism), which is so dear to all the tribes, should be revived, strengthened and practised in the true spirit of self-denial. Tribes should endeavour to be shining examples of enlightenment in their own spheres of influences.

References

Awnzagen, T (2012): *Shaikham,* (Churachandpur).

Bengal Eastern Frontier Regulation 1873.

Carey, Berthram S and HN Tuck (1983): *The Chin Hills* (New Delhi: Cultural Publishing House), 1, first published 1896.

Foreigners (Restricted Area) Order 1963.

Khobung, Vanthangpui (2013): IPEDR, 31 2012, IACSIT, Press Singapore, available at www. "http://www.google.com/url?q=h ttp%3A%2F%2Fetlibrary.org&sa= D&sntz= 1&usg=A FQjCNHBvCTtUbob49POOLukN28OSjSlVA" *etlibrary.org,* viewed on 25th January 2013.

Robert, TH (2008): "The British North-East Frontier Policy", available at *www.kukiforum.com,* viewed on 28th July 2012.

Sanga, R (2012): "The Manipur (Village Authority in Hill Areas) Act, 1956", available at *http://zogamonline.com/columns/r-sanga/14001-the-manipur-village-authority-in-hill-areas-act-1956.html,* viewed on 8th December 2012.

The Government of India (Excluded and Partially Excluded Areas) Order, 1936.

The Manipur Hill Areas (Acquisition of Chiefs' Rights) Act 1967.

The Manipur Hill Areas District Council Act, 1971 (as amended).

The Manipur Legislative Assembly Hill Areas Committee Order 1972.

The Manipur State Constitution Act 1947.

The Manipur State Hill Peoples (Administration) Regulation 1947.

The Manipur Village Authorities (in Hill Areas) Act 1956.

14

Challenges of Democratisation Process in India's North-East

Ginlianlal Buhril

This paper aims to provide a review of recent trends in the challenges faced in the democratisation process in India's North-East (NE) as well as discuss the significance of the case study of the Zomi community who have surmounted all odds, their struggle and success and how they could safeguard their ways of life, culture and fulfill their socio-economic and political aspirations. An analysis of the recent historical and management literature was carried out focussing on the benefits of a greater information access. By providing recommendations on how to progress further in a far more logical, systematic and appropriate manner, the paper assertively calls for a shift in perspective. That is, focus must be on the self, others, society and business. And that better leadership and governance can be learned.

Much is expected from this great community known to the world as the Zomis. How they have survived and progressed to claim their place in the sun deserved to be written down in history in letters of gold. How the winds and storms of life have hardened their mental, physical, emotional and spiritual resolve and have helped them achieve many successes almost in all walks of life would forever etched in the minds of all generation to come.

Overview of the Zomi Sub-nation

Quoting Harry Lee Kuan Yew, mentor and maker of modern Singapore, "Mine is a very matter-of-fact approach to the problem. If you can select a population and they are educated and they are properly brought up, then they do not have to use too much of the stick because they would already have been trained...I started off believing all men are equal. I now know that's the most unlikely thing ever to have been because millions of years have passed over evolution, people have scattered across the face of this earth, been isolated from each other, developed independently, had different intermixtures races, people, watching, arguing, asking and then bullying my way to the top that is the conclusion I've come to".

The term *"Zo"* is derived from the Zo king of the Zhou dynasty (B.C. 1027-225) of China. These were times the names of the ruling dynasty became the identity for the subjects. Zomis lived in Chin state in Myanmar and the Indian states of Manipur, Mizoram, Nagaland, Assam, Meghalaya, Arunachal Pradesh and all states of the NE. From a warrior clan to a temporary and deviant era of head-hunting and now a vibrant and enterprising citizens of the world, their transition have been significantly amazing, world-class and progress of the highest degree.

Common derivation from the generic name *"Zo"* could be in the form of using *Zou, Zhou, Chou, Shou, Yo, Jo, Yaw, Shu* in their speech and of words such as *"Zolei", "Zogam/Zoram", "Zotui", "Zofa"* in poetic language, and in naming geographical names such as *"Zotlang", "Zopui", "Zoutung", "Zobawks", "Zophei", "Zokhua", "Bawmzo"* and *"Zote".*

Zomi means Zo people. Zomis are the tribal plain people of Burma, Bangladesh and India as Chin, Kuki and Lushai. They are called Zomis because they are descendants of their great ancestor *"Zo"*. Fan-Cho, a diplomat of the Tang dynasty of China in 862 A.D., mentioned a kingdom in the Chindwin valley "whose princes and chiefs were called Shou or *Zo*". Father Vincentius Sangermano (1783) wrote in his book, *A*

Description of the Burmese Empire, a petty nation called *Jo* (*Jaw*). Henry Yule (1508) mentioned the *Yo* country, west of the Chindwin River. Howard Malcolm wrote about the Yaw (Zo) from the district *Yo*. Hence, the generic name *"Zo"* is the progenitor of the Zomi.

T.H. Lewin wrote during the Lushai Expedition (1871-72), "the generic name of the whole nation is Dzo". Francis Buchanan wrote extensively of the Zomi and their language. Pemberton mentioned *Zo* and *Jo* (1835) in his "Reports on the eastern frontiers of British India". G.A. Grierson argued in his writings that Zomis were known as *Zou* or *YO* or *Yaw* before the society evolved into clan-based organisation and lineage segmentation. "The name (Kuki and Chin) is not used by the tribes themselves, who use titles such as *Zou* or *Yo* or *Cho"*. U Thein Re Myint, a well-known Burmese writer who knew Chin history, perhaps even better than the Chin people themselves, wrote, "Even though those tribes of people, who are called Chin do not necessarily protest their name, their original name is, in fact, Zomi".

Bertram S. Carey and H.N. Tuck, two British administrators who were instrumental in placing Zo people under modern system of administration, record as follows: "Those of the Kuki tribes which we designate as Chins do not recognise that name. They call themselves *Yo* (Zo). *Yo* is the general name by which the Chins called their race". The European writer J. George Scott claimed that Zomi never called themselves by "the names like Kuki or Chin" or the "names given by their neighbours...Like others, the people do not accept the name given by the Burmese and ourselves. They call themselves Chin, and they equally flout the name of Kuki, which their Assamese neighbours used. They also call themselves Zhou or Shu and in others *Yo* or *Lai"*.

Without any doubt, *Zo* is indeed the ancestor of the Zo people. Modern Zo scholars and writers who have forcefully subscribe to this historical truth are T. Gougin, Khup Za Go, Vum Kho Hau, Vum Son, Lal Dena, Mangkhosat Kipgen,

Holngam Haokip, V. Lungnema, J.M. Paupu, H. Kamkhenthang, Lalthanliana, Tualchin Neihsial, Khen Za Sian, S. Prim Vaiphei, S.T. Hau Go, L. Keivom, L.S. Gangte, K. Zawla, R. Vanlawma, Thang Za Tuan, Sing Ling. All of these scholars and writers concluded that *Zo* is the ancestor of the Zo people.

Challenge of Seeing the "Big Picture"

The greatest challenge for the Zomis towards the democratisation process is seeing the big picture. The radical change the Zomis displayed, the paradigm shift that they have undergone made them a sub-nation in transition. To quote Pulitzer prize-winning journalist Thomas Friedman, author of *The World is Flat* and *The Lexus and the Olive Tree*, "Like everyone else trying to adjust to this new globalisation system and bring into focus, I had to retrain myself and develop new lenses to see it. Today, more than ever, the very traditional boundaries between politics, culture, technology, finance, national security and national security, and ecology are disappearing. You often cannot explain one without referring to the others, and you cannot explain the whole without reference to them at all. I wish I could say I understood all this when I began my career, but I didn't. I came to this approach entirely by accident, as successive changes in my career kept forcing me to add one more lens on top of another, just to survive".

Professor of Theoretical Physics at Caltech, Murray Gell-Mann states, "We need a corpus of people who consider that it is important to take a serious and very professional look at the whole system. It has to be a crude look because you will never master every part or every inter-connection. Unfortunately, in a great many places in our society, including academia and most bureaucracies, prestige accrues principally to those who study carefully some aspect of a problem, a trade, a technology or a culture". He continued, "We have to learn to have specialists and even generalists who could spot the strong interactions and entanglements of the different dimensions, and then take a crude look at the while".

Challenge of Continuing being a Society of Equals

Enterprise and consistency – the absence of contradictions-have been the hallmark of the Zomis. In relation to the mainstream India, in the historical not-so-long ago, they have at times felt marginalised. Here again, it must be accepted with a sense of maturity and truth that it was only a phase of getting to know each other better, each one having a demon to hover around and deceive. Since time immemorial, Zomis have always been aware of who they were. Theirs was and shall continue to be a society of equals. Naturally and in essence for a community with such rich heritage, democratic assimilation would always be easier.

Challenge of Continuing being a Community Known for its Creativity

The Zomis are known for their creativity and innovation bent of mind. Explore and examine their farming practices and wooden and bamboo propelled handicrafts and you would be more than impressed with this great sub-nation of Asia. Zomis are always socially responsible. "Social responsibility implies bringing corporate behaviour up to a level where it is congruent with the prevailing social norms, values and expectations" (Sethi 1975: 62). As a moral community, Zomis centred their operational and working lifestyle on the principle of respect (Bowie 2002). For the Zomis, the principle of respect entails the positive obligation to provide meaningful work-specify duties and provide leeway in determining how they are accomplished. For them, meaningful work is characterised by respect for autonomy, adequate wage and foregoing paternalism. Autonomy is recognised through democratic mechanism that permits all involved parties to have a voice in workplace governance.

Challenge of Continuing being a Responsible and Self-sufficient Economy

Since time immemorial, the Zomis were known to be highly responsible as individuals and as a community. They stand for workplace democracy. Known for its own self-sufficient village economy where individuals and families freely share with their neighbours articles and economic products rather than commercialised them, the issue facing us now is how best to collaborate and continue this significant tradition. If there is a community that would be capable of going global beyond the local operations, it would be the Zomi community. The future augurs well for this great community known as Zomis of Asia.

Challenge of the Human Resources Management

High standardised accessibility to latest technology has propelled the Zomis to become a community of software and technology practitioners. They loved to cross territorial borders and boundaries to blend with the Indian and international societies. In terms of assimilation to the Indian mainstream, in terms of socialisation of society and in process of democratisation, they would be one of the fastest progressive sub-nations in the Indian continent. What makes us think that the Zomis could market themselves for the future could understandably be responded as; Zomis could define and understand reality of market. They could learn from their failures. They could treasure the people who would be customers.

Challenge of Existing in Tune with the World

Success of pastoral Churches and the capabilities of members to exploit demographic changes as marketing opportunity are significant trends in the Zomi society. The Zomis are always known to foresee opportunities early and seize them, focus on individual's need for a free, integrated community giving full responsibilities to members. Individual's spiritual needs in the Zomi community forms a great unifying and bonding societal and religious practices. Hindering factors for growth and handicaps for progress would all be slowly surmounted. In essence, people's practices, performances and productivity would be ensured to become more effective.

Challenge of Governance

Much could be desired when it comes to leadership and skillful governance showed by leaders of the Zomis. Positive deviants (Sternin and Marsh 1998), and their respect for the right of association and the manner in which they could find better solutions to a problem than their peers, despite having no special resources or knowledge are the rare competitive advantage leaders of the Zomis displayed as a reflection of their values. This insight is worth preserving and still relevant to modern life and for democratisation process in India's NE region. Governance shifts seen now is from domestic to a global logic (Koenig-Archibugi 2004; Schulte 2005). This is an authentic democratisation process in full bloom and of the rarest kind wherein governance is even beyond the state, yet in a globalising world where the increasing mobility and flow of people, goods and services is rendering borderless relevant with nation-states increasingly inter-connected politically, socially and economically (Habermas 1998; Henderson, Dicken, Hess, Coe., and Young 2002). The same governance shifts is causing a denationaliation of various political issues (Zurn 2004).

Challenge of Nurturing Character-based Virtues

The Zomis are reflective people. They understand that the right to life imposes a correlative duty on the community to make provision for those who cannot adequately feed or clothe themselves. The Zomis in the 21st century stand for strong character.

Challenge of Educating Every Girl

Possibly this could be one of the greatest challenges for the democratisation process of the NE in the years to come. Education for the girl child cause is honourable, necessary leading to empowerment of women and growth of the nation. The hand that rocks the cradle rules the world and it is important that every girl be educated for the Zomi society to progress and accelerate their democratisation process. The girl child and women in the Zomi community hold the key to whatever progressive achievement visible to behold.

Discussion

How does one think of the future of the Zomis in terms of business, principles, competition, control and complexity, leadership, and in terms of marketing themselves in the world that is competitive, technology driven, result-oriented and so very customer-oriented? What would the future hold for this enterprising community? Our attempt at answering these questions so relevant that they all are shall be based on the ideas and thoughts and of course contributions of contemporary modern management *gurus*. We need to rethink to shape our future before it shapes us as a community.

Rethinking Principles

Stephen Covey says, "Putting principles first". Charles Handy says, "Finding sense in uncertainty". Tomorrow's successful leaders will value principles more than they value their companies (Covey). We are talking about principle-centred leaders, high trust culture, belief in human potential, principles in practice when times get tough. The leader in the Zomi community must continue to function like the farmer who could create the right conditions and the right climate for growth.

Rethinking Competition

Michael Porter says, "Creating tomorrow's advantages". C.K. Prahalad calls it "strategies for growth". Gary Hamel calls it "reinventing the basis for competition". Michael Porter's words are, "The important thing is to try to shape the nature of competition, to take control over our own destiny. It is not just a matter of being better at what you do; it is a matter of being different at what you do". Be it the importance of innovation, the role of technology, technology versus innovation, the fact is that new technology always sweep away potential advantages. Competing for the future means maintaining continuity by constantly creating new sources of profit (Prahalad). The great excitement of the future is that we shape it (Handy).

Charles Doughnut Principle states, "Life is like an inverted doughnut in which the hole is on the outside and the dough is in the middle. In the doughnut view of life, the core is fixed and the bounded space around the core is where we make the main difference. The core gives us the bit of security and certainty which we all need, while the space gives us the flexibility". You cannot stumble backwards into the future (Handy). Creating tomorrow advantages means finding ways of growing and building advantages rather than just eliminating disadvantages (Porter).

Rethinking the Basis for Competition

Gary Hamel's words are, "You cannot create the future using the old strategy tools".

Rethinking Control and Complexity

Michael Hammer calls it, "Beyond the end of management". Eli Goldraft calls this "focussing on constraints, not cost". To quote Peter Senge, "Through the eye of the needle we have to start the premise that that what we need is high-performing processes". The goal is not to save money but to make money. If pure common sense violates the rules that exist, then you have to conclude that the rules that exist are not common sense, but very common nonsense. We have to develop a sense of connectedness, a sense of working together as part of a system where each part of a system is affecting and being affected by the others, and where the whole is greater than the sum of its parts, so says the great management guru of the 21st Century, Peter Senge.

Rethinking Leadership

Warren Bennis calls it "process of becoming a core leader of leaders". John Kotter calls it "cultures and coalitions".

"What leaders must learn to do is to develop a social architecture that encourages incredibly bright people, most of whom have big egos, to work together successfully and to deploy their own creativity". "The major challenge for leaders in the 21st century will be, of course be how to release the brainpower of their organisations".

Rethinking Cultures and Coalitions

Quoting John Kotter: "Do we have corporate cultures that are anchors on change? Or cultures that enable us to adapt to the main changing environment?"

Rethinking Markets and Mapping the Future

Al Ries and Jack Trout call this "Focussed in a fuzzy world" and Philip Kotler himself coined the term "mapping the future market place". Soon, and very soon, the Zomis would start restyling themselves as networks of entrepreneurs. Previously, the more tribal they are the more local they become. Now, the more universal they become, the more tribal they act. As the Zomi community becomes increasingly "boundaryless", distributed and even networked, the Zomi culture would immensely benefit. The Zomis are now rethinking positioning. An entertainment explosion is happening to the community. The community has emerged to be high-income consumers. The community has step-up in the areas of quality and service orientation.

To quote the words of Philip Kotler, "Tomorrow's winners will be those that lead their industry in targetting their markets carefully and producing the best value for money in those target markets". As a community that is vibrant, enterprising, industrious, forward looking and very accommodative to new ideas, the above statement should hold true for the Zomis of NE India.

Learning from the Gurus

Prahalad says, "Competing for the future is not merely about having foresight". He also says, "Redundant manpower to be used to build new core competencies that would give them an advantage in the market". "Downsizing can make you leaner and thinking, but it won't necessarily make you healthier".

Ed Artzt states, "If we don't do it early on globally someone else will".

Gary Hamel says, "Simply catching up to where others have been is necessary to stay in the game, but I believe that the winners will ultimately be those with the real ability to invent fundamentally new games". "You have to create a deep sense of restlessness with the status quo". "Democratisation of strategy is crucial". "If you want to create a point of view about the future, if you want to craft a meaningful strategy, you have to create in your community a hierarchy of imagination".

Michael Hammer says, "If you think you are good, you are dead". "Every individual on the team is focussed on the objective, which involves cooperating with others while carrying out your own particular set of duties". "Customers have come to expect that we do things their way, rather than that they do things our way".

Warren Bennis says, "Tomorrow leaders will have to learn how to create an environment that actually embraces change, not as a threat but as an opportunity".

Peter F Drucker in his book, *Managing for the Future: The 1990s and Beyond* (1992: 93), talks about the new productivity challenge as "Productivity and effectiveness in making and moving things – in government services, corporate world, academics, military service and information technology". "There are really two demands of leadership. One is to accept that rank does not confer privileges; it entails that congruence between deeds and words, between behaviour and professed beliefs and values, that we called 'personal integrity".

Tom Peter in his book, *Thriving on Chaos. Handbook for Management Revolution* (1987), says, "Three outstanding attitudes – obliviousness to the growing disaffection of constituents, primacy of self-aggrandisement and illusion of invulnerable status – are persistent aspects of folly".

Research Implications

Our paper allows for multiple avenues of future theoretical and empirical research. We need to think beyond certainty, learn to live with chaos and uncertainty. We need to give society a mind of its own. The enemy is us and our own societies because what we are fighting against is our own sense of values, our own principles. A fresh look at competitive strategy and the pitfalls in strategic thinking is required. Strategic architecture and de-risking opportunities as well as unlearning the past would greatly help. Rethinking competition and creating incentives are the challenges. Personal development, cultural differences are fertile areas for 21st century research. Rethinking hierarchies is required. The 21st century leadership and creating a guiding coalition are both significantly capable of causing an impact of great magnitude.

John Kotter says, "It is only through leadership that you can truly develop and nurture a culture that is adaptive to change". "Of course, the best way to handle culture is to never let it get broken in the first place to interrupt the syndrome by never letting it get to the point where you end up with an arrogant, internally focussed, centralised and bureaucratic culture". Al Ries and Jack Trout states, "Conceptually, the bigger the market, the more specialised you have to become if you want to succeed". Philip Kotler says, "Marketers will move from focussing on large segments to targetting specific niches. In niches there are riches".

Recommendation and Conclusion

Patience is the call of the hour. What facilitates the growth most are the forces that act against it. My recommendation and conclusion based on the views expressed shall be at two levels. First, democratisation process of the NE is slowly, surely and certainly and significantly getting better and better. Our case examination of the Zomi community progress on all fronts has openly proved and endorsed this gospel truth. Performance of human resources is up qualitatively and quantitatively. Attention on market-oriented economy is impressive. Technology assimilative contributions are noteworthy, not much cause for worry on leadership and governance with the huge number of top talents coming into the profession. Education in itself is a very strong vehicle of progress and of course great women empowerment – all are life transforming achievements.

Secondly, the thinking and rethinking for the future in terms of principles, business, competition, control and complexity, leadership, markets and the world are well-focussed. Networks are up and on the rise. The Zomis themselves are a nation on the move. A great star on the horizon of the new world. The beauty is that this is only the beginning of greater things to come. Perhaps, the Zomi model could be used as a classic example for other communities in NE India. John Naisbitt was right when he wrote *From Nation States to Network,* and said my one-word message for the 21st Asia – a corrected version would be "India in Asia" and for us the reality would be the Zomis in India's NE.

References

Adam, RM (1999): *A Theory of Virtue: Excellence in being for the Good* (New York: Oxford University Press).

Anderson, C (1997): "Values-based Management", *Academy of Management Executive*, 11(4): 25.

Arya, B and JE Salk (2006): "Cross Sector Alliance Learning and Effectiveness of Voluntary Codes of Corporate Social Responsibility", *Business Ethics Quarterly*, 16: 211-34.

Audi, R (2004): *The Good in the Right* (Princeton, N.J.: Princeton University Press).

Baron, David P (1996): *Business and its Environment* (New Jersey: Prentice Hall).

Bowie, NE (1999): *Business Ethics: A Kantian Perspective* (Oxford: Blackwell Publishers).

Budd, JW (2004): *Employment with a Human Face: Balancing Efficiency, Equity, and Voice* (Ithaca, N.Y.: ILR Press).

C. Dalton, D (2003): "Conflicts of Interest: A Corporate Governance Pitfall", *The Journal of Business Strategy*, 24(4): 7.

Chakroborty, Kiran Sankar and Gurudas Das eds. (2006): *Human Development: Experiences of North-East India* (New Delhi: Akansha Publishing House).

Davis, K and RL Blomstrom eds. (1971): *Business, Society, and Environment: Social Power and Social Response* (New York: McGraw-Hill), second ed.

Doris, JM (2002): *Lack of Character: Personality and Moral Behaviour* (New York: Cambridge University Press).

Drucker, P (1978): *Management: Tasks, Responsibilities, Practices* (New York: Harper and Row).

Drucker, P (1989): *The New Realities* (New York: Harper and Row).

Drucker, Peter F (1992): *Managing for the Future: The 1990s and Beyond* (New York: Penguin Books Ltd.).

Greenleaf, R (1993): *Stewardship: Choosing Service and Self-interest* (San Francisco: Berrett-Koehler Publishers).

Hamel, G (2000): *Leading the Revolution* (Cambridge, MA: Harvard Business School Press).

Keynes, JM (1973): *The General Theory of Employment, Interest and Money* (London: Macmillan).

Moore, G (2012): "The Virtue of Governance, the Governance of Virtue", *Business Ethics Quarterly*, 22: 293-318.

Nash, L (1990): *Good Intentions Aside: A Manager's Guide to Resolving Ethical Problems* (Boston: Harvard Business School).

Nayak, P (2010): *Human Development Reports in North-East India: A Bird's Eye View*, MPRA Paper No. 17013.

Reave, L (2005): "Spiritual Values and Practices Related to Leadership Effectiveness", *The Leadership Quarterly*, 16: 655-687.

Rokeach, M (1973): *The Nature of Human Values* (New York: Free Press).

Zagzebski, L (2001): "The Uniqueness of Persons", *The Journal of Religious Ethics*, 29(3): 401-23.

15

Tribal Land Issues with Reference to Manipur

R. Sanga

Introduction

The affinity of tribal people with the forest was aptly described by Elwin (1963) as, "exploiting its products they can supplement their meager income. It keeps them warm and does family chores and constructs their houses. Their religion leads them to believe that there are many spirits living in the trees. There are special sacrifices to the forest gods. In many places, offerings are made to a tree before it is cut down and there are usually ceremonies before and after hunting". To the tribal people, the forest is their sweet home, their livelihood and their very existence. It gives them food, fruits of all kinds, edible leaves, honey, nourishing roots, fish and wild game. Tribal legends and mythologies speak of their relation with forests and sylvan spirits. From ancient to recent times, the tribal people are enjoying the freedom of using the forest and hunt the animals. This has given to them the conviction that remains in their hearts, even today that the forest belongs to them.

There have been many discussions on the issue of tribal lands in Manipur. The tribal land ownership system of Manipur is based on the customs, cultures and traditions of the tribes. There is no uniform land use pattern. The land use pattern in the hill areas of Manipur is in the nature of shifting cultivation, wet cultivation and homestead of village settlement. The hill area of Manipur, which covers an area of 20,126 sq. km. out of the geographical area of 22,326 sq. km., was under chiefship since time immemorial. This institution with the help of the village authority fragmented all tribal lands as per the capacity of the different chiefs of different communities or clans. The Nagas and the Zo indigenous peoples in the hill areas of Manipur strictly adhered to their system. They are so sensitive to their existing system that they disdain any slight change for improvement or suggestion. Simultaneously, there is no constitutional provision to safeguard their system which they firmly cling to it as their birth right.

A Brief Historical Background of the Administration of the Hill Areas

From the pre-and post-British colonial period, hill areas of Manipur were administered separately. Traditional laws and customs of the different tribes are the basis of administration and this continued with whimsical changes for all intents and purposes, even after India gained independence.

With the introduction of the Government of India Act 1935, the then principality of Manipur immediately joined the negotiation for hammering out the terms of federation with the Government of India. One of the main subjects of controversy was the administration of the hills of Manipur. The British adjudged it unsafe to leave the administration of the hill areas within the jurisdiction of the then Manipur durbar. After a lengthy negotiation on 21st July 1939, the Maharajah of Manipur agreed, "to federate on terms which covered the exclusion of the hills from his direct control". The signing of the standstill agreement and the instrument of accession on the same day on 11th August 1947, and the merger agreement on 21st September 1949, through which the Manipur principality became part of the Indian republic did not change this scheme of governance.

In the sixties when the demand for the territory of Manipur to be converted into a full-fledged state was gaining momentum, the need for maintaining a separate administration for the tribals was acknowledged. From 1967 onwards, the drafting process for a law applicable to the hill areas of Manipur commenced. The Parliament of India enacted the Manipur (Hill Areas) District Council Act on 26th December 1971. The Act among others established six autonomous district councils in Manipur. On 21st January 1972, Manipur became a full-fledged state. The Manipur Legislative Assembly (Hill Areas Committee) Order, 1972 was made on 20th June 1972 by the then President of India, V.V. Giri. Subsequently, in exercising of its rule making powers, the Government of Manipur through the Governor framed the Manipur Autonomous District Council (Election of Members) Rules, 1972 to facilitate the process of electing council members. The Rules of 1972 governed the election process and no alterations were made to the Rules until 2010.

The Manipur Government is now trying to meddle with the independent functioning of the Hill Areas Committee by a cabinet decision to institute a committee to reorganise the district boundaries and police jurisdictions in the entire state. Committee on reorganisation of administrative and police boundary was formed in connection with Sadar Hill District and Jiribam Revenue District Demand Committees' agitations in which the Chief Secretary D.S. Poonia acts as its chairman.

Revenue Commissioner will be the convener of the committee while Director General of Police, Manipur, Principal Secretary RD & PR and Commissioner of Home and Hills will be the members of the committee (Hueiyen Lanpao 2011). Neither a single tribal leader was nominated as member of the committee nor was hill areas committee consulted in this regard. It is apprehension that the said committee will conduct land survey under the MLR and LR Act, 1960. While this may serve the interests of the plain people, it will greatly affect indigenous tribal lands system of Manipur.

The Manipur State Hill People (Administration) Regulation, 1947

To make the issue clearer, let us look back the Manipur State Hill People (Administration) Regulation, 1947. Before application of any land law in Manipur, the Raja of Manipur claimed absolute ownership of all lands within his territory in the valley area and collected land revenue. On the other hand, during the British period, the administration of the entire hill areas of Manipur was under the responsibility of the President of Manipur durbar who was a British ICS officer. The hill areas were separately administered as per a set of rules known as the Manipur State Hill People (Administration) Regulation, 1947. The hill areas were at no point of time under the administration of the Raja of Manipur. The administration was carried on to the tune of the hill peoples' aspirations and their age-old customs and traditional practices.

In 1952, a new national forest policy in India added further restrictions on tribal peoples. Under the old policy, the forestland could be released for cultivation subject to certain safeguards and free grazing was allowed. The new policy barred cultivation but allowed grazing on payment. Elwin (1963) very aptly depicts the position of the tribal people in the changed circumstances. Thus, the tribal who regarded himself as the lord of the forests was through a deliberate process turned into a subject and placed under the forest department. Tribal villages were no longer an essential part of the forests but were there merely on sufferance. The traditional rights of the tribals were no longer recognised as rights. In 1894, they became "rights and privileges" and in 1952, they became "rights and concessions". Now, they are regarded as "concessions". The tribals take this as denigrating.

While such was the considered administration for hill/tribal people, a land Act was enacted in 1960, which had rather frightened the tribals with the land being alienated from them. Unfortunately, the Manipur State Hill People (Administration) Regulation, 1947 had been repealed in part by Section 58 of the Manipur (Village Authorities in Hill Areas) Act, 1956 (80 of 1956) without obtaining referendum from the tribal peoples of Manipur, nor the then tribal leaders were consulted before repealing it. I am afraid that all the privileges and rights of the Manipur tribal may be deprived of by the repealed of the said Regulation.

Tribal/Indigenous Peoples' Rights with Regards to Lands, Forest and Natural Resources

The United Nations Conference on Environment and Development (the East Summit) held in Brazil in 1992 represents a turning point in the promotion of indigenous peoples' right relating to the environment. The Earth Summits such as the Rio declaration, agenda 21 and the convention on biological diversity establish international legal standard to protect indigenous peoples' rights to their traditional knowledge and practices in the area of environmental management and conservation. Most importantly, now, there exists an international legal framework, which recognises the unique relationship of indigenous people to have their traditional lands.

The provisions of the UN Declaration on the Rights of Indigenous Peoples that are applicable to the tribal land use and system in the hill areas of Manipur are cited below:

Article 3: Indigenous peoples have the right to self-determination. By virtue of that right, they freely determine their political status and freely pursue their economic, social and cultural development.

Article 15: The right of the peoples concerned to the natural resources pertaining to their lands shall be specially safeguarded. These rights include the right of these peoples to participate in the use, management and conservation of their resources.

Article 28: Indigenous peoples have the right to maintain and strengthen their distinctive spiritual and material relationship with land, territories, rivers and coastal seas and other resources, which they have traditionally owned or occupied or used, and to uphold their responsibility to future generations in this regard.

Article 31: Indigenous peoples as a specific form of exercising their right to self-determination, have the right to autonomy or self-determination in matters relating to their internal and local affairs including culture, religion, educations, information, media, health, housing, employment, social welfare, economic activities, land and resources management, environment and enter by new members, as well as ways and means for financing these autonomous functions.

Indigenous Peoples and Tribal Land Issues in the North-East India

Before the conquest and annexation of the tribal areas of North-East (NE) India, the sovereign authority of each village under the chiefs existed without any outside interference. The chiefs ruled over their people/villagers in accordance with their own customs, cultures and tradition. The chiefs collected revenue/tax in kind from each household in the villages. Chiefs of each village looked after the cultivation and were responsible for realisation of tax payable by each cultivator. However, members of the chief's council were exempted from tax payment. In short, the tribal chiefs are "lord of the soil" within their respective jurisdiction.

The properties of the villagers were protected and their institutions of administrative machinery under the chiefs were fully preserved during the pre-British period. Education makes a man, so goes the saying. Though the tribals had no education during the pre-British days, they had a novel way of governing their people. Kinship ties were strong. Social institutions were well utilised by them. It was mandatory on all tribal youths over 15 years of age to stay in bachelor dormitories known as *"haam"*, or *"zawlbuk"*, which was one of the most important social institutions amongst the tribal peoples, where they received training in "tribal warfare, wrestling, hunting and village government". The training was intensive and strenuous. Strict discipline was maintained. In other words, the bachelor dormitory was an institution where the young tribal males not only picked up skills in self-defense but also developed a positive attitude to life.

During the colonial period, the tribal areas were divided into different circles, merely to fit the colonial administrative convenience. Each circle was kept under a colonial political agent. It was the same in the case of Manipur. The British consolidated and respected the rights and traditional institutions in the entire hill areas of Manipur. The properties of the tribal of Manipur were so attached to the authority of the chief that none can disturb it. Further, in the matter of administration of justice and trial of cases, the political agent was given the power over the hill tribes.

Need for Development through Institutional Finance

The policy about tribal development after independence was that of adopting a middle path—between the two extremes of complete insulation and free play of economic forces. In the words of Pandit Jawaharlal Nehru, "We cannot allow matters to drift in the tribal area..." He desired that the people should be allowed to develop along the lines of their genius. The task had to be performed through their own social and cultural institutions without overwhelming them with the maze of the modern economic institutions. A great concern was also shown on the cultural heritage of the tribals. To quote Pandit Gobind Ballabh Pant, "The tribals should develop their own culture and make their contribution to the cultural richness of the country. It is unnecessary to cause them to change their customs, habits or diversions so much as to make them indistinguishable from the other classes..."

There are no formalised institutions. The tentacles of administration and economic institutions, by and large, may not have reached these areas. Even when they reached, their significance is hardly appreciated. Gradually these areas are coming within the effective purview of modern formalised institutional system. The tribal community has no full understanding of the new formal system. The legal frame which is the source of all formal authority is a great mystery to the tribal.

Considering these economic systems and social organisations of the tribals, the developmental strategy for all-round improvement should be planned. In this regard, the National Commission on Agriculture, 1976 stated that the development of hill areas has to be planned within the framework of an articulated long-term plan in which the sources of development programmes are adequately balanced by essential infrastructural facilities, particularly communications and minimum social development programme from traditional pattern to those suitable for hill development. It requires a concentrated effort in research investigation and particularly in formulation of viable projects. In the past, development efforts in hill areas were frustrated by project gaps.

It is now recognised by the planners that a comprehensive and integrated development plan involving different discipline is required to tackle the problems of the tribal communities. The idea of preparing sub-plans for tribal areas out of the consolidated fund of India under Article 275 of the Constitution of India, and of the project approach to formulating and implementing integrated programmes on viable area basis is, therefore, basically sound and should be commended. There will be a need to adopt the sub-plans to each specific project area varying the emphasis on different elements according to local problems and potentialities.

Conclusion

The tribal people of Manipur, from primeval ages have been under the leadership of their chiefs. The chiefs are the custodians of tribal culture and customs. The tribal people are protected through the chiefs. The tribal chiefs of Manipur hold title and own the village land under their jurisdiction. They share the land with their villagers. Thus, a sustainable tribal economy evolves out of this practice.

It is well-known that the sole duty of the Hill Areas Committee in Manipur is to look after the special interests of the tribal peoples of the state according to the provisions enshrined in the Constitution of India under Article 371C. Highest priority has to be given to the land problem. The tribals have lost land to a large extent through alienation. Although there is legislation against the transfer of tribal land, various ingenious devices have been employed to circumvent the law. Before a meaningful programme of land development can be taken up, it is necessary that the lands which have already passed from their hands are to be restored to them. The existing laws and rules must be reviewed to plug any loophole and give adequate protection to the tribals under the constitutional provision.

In today's globalising world, the concerns of indigenous peoples can no longer be ignored or suppressed. They have become better organised and capable of demanding equality in sharing benefits from development projects in both national and international forums. They are searching for ways to overcome obstacles to the eradication of their poverty and underdevelopment (Gonzalez-Parra 2001). "Indigenous peoples have dynamic living cultures and seek their place in the modern world. They are not against development, but for too long, they have been victims of development and now demand to be the participants in—and to benefit from—a development that is sustainable" (Magga 2004).

References

1989: *The International Labour Organisation and Indigenous and Tribal Peoples,* ILO Convention Concerning Indigenous and Tribal Peoples, Leaflet No. 169.

Basu, Durga Das (1989): *Shorter Constitution of India* (New Delhi: Prentice-Hall of India Pvt. Ltd.), tenth ed.

Devi, P Binodini (2006): *Tribal Land System of Manipur* (Imphal: Centre for Manipur Studies, Manipur University).

Government of Manipur Law Department, *A Hand Book of Manipur Hill Village Authority. A Compilation of the Manipur (Village Authority in this Areas) Act, 1956 and Rules framed thereunder including Notifications issued under the Act and Rules No. 178/26.8.71. C/2,000* (Imphal: Government Press).

Rules of Procedure and Conduct of Business in Manipur Legislative Assembly (Imphal: Manipur Legislative Assembly Secretariat), eight ed.

The Manipur Hill Areas District Councils Act, 1971 and Rules, 1972, Government of Manipur, Planning and Development Department, Imphal, 9th March 1972.

Index

C

F

G

H

I